# Marketing Your Products and Services Successfully

## By Harriet Stephenson
## Dorothy Otterson

• OASIS PRESS •

Published by Oasis Press*
720 South Hillview Drive
Milpitas, California 95035
    408/263-9671

International Standard Book Number - 0-916378-32-2
                    Paper - 0-916378-83-7

Printed in the United States of America

10 9 8 7 6 5 4 3 2


*Division of Publishing Services, Inc. a Texas corporation.

# Contents

# Introduction

This book is intended to serve as a consultant and interactive marketing planner for the small business entrepreneur who is introducing a new product or service into the marketplace. The concepts and exercises work equally as well for an established business person who intends to expand his or her service offering or product line. Completing the worksheets will help you succeed in selling your product or service at a profit.

Small business is the backbone of America. Did you know that of the 15 million businesses in existence in the United States in 1984, probably 97% could be classified as small? According to the Small Business Administration, however, only one in five startups remains in business after four or five years. This means that a great many businesses with high-quality products or services and good intentions don't succeed—mainly due to insufficient marketing and management skills.

Assuming you have good management skills, marketing a product or service begins with the need to have something you are enthused with—that you can believe in—that you feel good about promoting. It is also critical that people want or need your product or service and will pay a reasonable price for it. What you name the product or service, its price and quality, its function, how it is described or packaged—the shape, color, size—are all important aspects of the sale.

Various aspects of advertising—the slogan, the logo and symbols, ad content, print style, hidden message, border, white space, size, color, placement of the ad—can greatly impact the sales outcome. A good slogan can help increase sales, for example, by being easy or clever enough to generate word-of-mouth advertising at no extra cost to you. Location, building or facilities, service, hours of business, nature of competition, clientele, how the customer experiences the product or service and whether they refer it to others can also affect sales potential.

A good market-centered approach requires careful consideration of all these aspects to sell your product or service at a viable profit. Concentration on the following three-step marketing sequence can provide the structure for achieving marketing success.

1. **Identify your target market(s).**

   o What are you selling—goods or services?

   o At what life-cycle stage?

   o To whom are you selling?

   o What resources are available to help determine target market(s)?

   o Which research survey techniques are best for your case?

   o Where can you best locate your business?

   o What is your unique market?

   o What price are you asking?

2. **Develop and communicate awareness of your product or service.**

   o How do you let customers know that you have what they want?

   o What are the best packaging, price, and media alternatives?

   o Where and how can customers get the benefits?

3. **Deliver customer satisfaction**

   o Pre-delivery planning, selling, getting the order or contract.

   o Delivery of the product or production of the service.

   o Customer satisfaction builds success. This establishes customer results or payoff. The goal is to get the product or service to deliver benefits as promised and cultivate repeat business and referrals.

Through using the guidelines, examples, and worksheets presented here, the entrepreneur who wants an understandable and practical marketing approach is able to design a successful, personalized strategy.

## Utilizing this Interactive Resource

Successful marketing involves finding a need and filling it—at a profit—by providing desirable goods and services to satisfied customers. This interactive resource will guide you through the marketing process by asking questions to help determine your specific product or service niche (Chapter 1), your most likely target markets (Chapter 2), and an appropriate price (Chapter 3). Then develop a successful marketing campaign through total image packaging (Chapter 4), select the best advertising media and sales promotions (Chapter 5) and establish a workable budget (Chapter 6). Once your marketing campaign is underway, delivering customer satisfaction (Chapter 7) is essential to remain in business. In fact, once successful, you may eventually want to expand your marketing effort to include other parts of the United States and abroad (Chapter 8).

Perhaps a useful approach to getting the best value from this book is to first overview the entire contents. If you are already marketing a product or service, utilize this workbook to help redefine current marketing strategy. You may need to review Chapter 4 on developing awareness of your product or service. Taking the time to fill in the various worksheets will give you a much clearer picture of your current marketing strategy. From this you will be able to determine marketing strengths and weaknesses and take positive action to ensure greater success for your current product or service offering.

If you are just starting out in a new business, familiarize yourself with the marketing terminology presented here. This book is organized into eight chapters that cover different aspects of the marketing process, including a chapter on international marketing. Each chapter presents marketing concepts, asks questions for your immediate response, and includes worksheets which summarize specific responses about your products or services. Many examples are included in the text to give you an idea how others have successfully marketed their products and services. The worksheets are designed to help quickly reference questions in the preceding text. This interactive process helps to reassure you that questions raised in the text are summarily answered in the worksheets. Worksheets generally begin on the righthand side of the page and do not have text on the reverse side if they are one page in length. The left-hand page preceding a worksheet is sometimes left blank so that the text more closely corresponds with the worksheet reference.

Your marketing strategy will evolve as you fill in all the worksheets. The combined worksheets will represent your marketing plan so that you can see whether you're on target or whether your marketing plan needs modification in one or more areas.

Appendixes are also included which support concepts presented in the text.

# Chapter 1
# Identifying Your Potential Target Market

It is necessary to begin any marketing program with yourself. Are you selling goods or services? What classifications of business do you have? What are conditions in your industry? This chapter will help you with these primary questions and also introduce you to some terms that are used throughout this book. The major purpose of classifying and describing your goods and services is to help identify prospective target markets. Goods can be identified according to basic use. Services will be discussed in the next section.

## Goods

**Industrial goods** are those products used in producing other goods, or intended for resale to the final user. Some examples are computer chips, leather, aluminum, and plastic. **Consumer goods** are those products intended for use by the ultimate consumer. Examples include personal computers, shoes, soft drinks in aluminum cans, and plastic rain gear. Of course, many products, such as nuts and bolts, foodstuffs, and chemicals, can be targeted for both industrial users and consumers. Since the buyer group may determine the nature of your advertising appeal and the medium through which the product or service is promoted, it is useful to classify your products.

```
Q1-1    My product is:
        __ an industrial good
        __ a consumer good
        __ both
```

Goods can be further differentiated according to buyer characteristics (Who? When? What? Where? How? Why?)

**Convenience goods** are products the industrial user or consumer wants to purchase frequently, immediately, and with a minimum of effort.

o These goods are usually low-priced and come under many brand names at numerous retail outlets for maximum buyer convenience.

o Promotion is usually the responsibility of the manufacturer.

o Marketing intermediaries (wholesalers and retailers) are commonly used.

o Examples include candy, chewing gum, milk, soft drinks, beer, nails, and small machinery parts.

**Shopping goods** are products purchased only after the industrial user or consumer has made comparisons of competing goods based on such factors as price, quality, style, color, brand, and image.

o These goods tend to be higher priced than convenience items.

o Promotion is often shared by manufacturer and retailer (perhaps through cooperative advertising).

o Examples include clothing, jewelry, furniture, appliances, cars.

**Specialty goods** are products which possess some unique characteristics that cause the buyer to prize that particular brand or style.

o By advertising unique qualities, manufacturers can command a higher price—often whatever the market will bear.

o Consumers and industrial users are willing to pay a high price, go out of their way, or wait a considerable time period to acquire these products.

o Manufacturers frequently use a small number of suppliers or retail outlets for each geographic area in their target market.

o Examples include original works of art, imported quality items, expensive sports cars, handmade furniture, and customized products.

| Q1-2 | My product can be further classified as: |
|---|---|
| | __ a convenience good |
| | __ a shopping good |
| | __ a specialty good |

**Classification by Product Characteristics.** The major purpose of classifying your product is to help zero in on your target market, especially with regard to tailoring your advertising appeals. You may wish to classify products according to descriptive characteristics such as the following.

o **Unit cost** (top of the line versus least expensive) affects the buying decision due to the price charged.

| Q1-3 Describe the product using relative unit cost criteria. |
|---|
| |

o **Energy spent** getting the item (little effort for convenience goods found most everywhere versus more time for expensive items for which the consumer or industrial user must shop around).

---

Q1-4 Classify your product using energy spent.

---

o **Importance or value** of the individual item to the consumer or industrial user (a pack of gum versus a car or house, a nut or bolt versus insulation material).

---

Q1-5 Describe the relative value of your product to its buyer.

---

o **Rate of change in technology or fashion** (a microcomputer versus a wooden pencil; the teenage clothing market versus fishing attire).

---

Q1-6 Describe how the rate of change in technology or fashion affects your product.

---

o **Amount of service or training needed** (before, during, and after buying a microcomputer versus a windup wristwatch).

Q1-7 Describe how much service or training is needed to use the product.

o **Frequency of purchase** (several times during one's life for a house versus daily or weekly for a quart of milk or newspaper).

Q1-8 Describe how frequently a customer is likely to purchase the product.

## Worksheet 1 Product Characteristics Summary

My product is purchased primarily by (consumers, industrial users, both) _____ (Q1-1) and can basically be classified as a (convenience, shopping, specialty) item (Q1-2).

Summarize your product characteristics by filling in the chart below.

|  | Low | Medium | High |  |
|---|---|---|---|---|
| 1. Unit cost |  |  |  | ( Q1-3) |
| 2. Energy spent |  |  |  | (Q1-4) |
| 3. Importance to buyer |  |  |  | (Q1-5) |
| 4. Rate of change |  |  |  | (Q1-6) |
| 5. Service or training |  |  |  | (Q1-7) |
| 6. Frequency of purchase |  |  |  | (Q1-8) |
| 7. Other |  |  |  |  |

## Services

The service sector of the economy accounts for almost 40 percent of total consumer expenditures. It also provides two-thirds of all private (non-government) jobs in the United States. As a result, service businesses represent a major growth sector, even in a "down" economy. It is relatively easy to start a service business with minimum capital invested. It's also easy to miss the target market unless you define it and actively go after it by promoting your services.

Service businesses such as real estate agencies, barbershops, dry cleaners, repair shops, and tax accounting firms are classified in various ways to help the service provider target a specific marketing segment for an advertising appeal. You could use the same product designations of "convenience," "shopping," and "specialty" to identify your service category. You might also classify according to characteristics such as the following:

o **Type of service specialty** (inventory consultant versus management consultant).

```
Q1-9 My service specialty is



```

o **Type of service provider** (academic class offerings versus private, nondegree classes).

```
Q1-10 The major provider type of my service is




```

o **Type of buyer** (military, government agency, private industry, nonprofit organization).

```
Q1-11 The major buyer type of my service is



```

Q1-12 My service, classified by service specialty, provider or buyer can be summarized as:

Another classification distinguishes the **instrumental** service provider versus the **expressive** service provider. In purchasing an instrumental service (i.e., one viewed as being a means to some other valued end), the user or consumer wants to minimize the time and cost involved in purchasing and using or consuming it. For example, "Let's aim for the quickest, nearest, cheapest, fast-food place. I'm starving and I surely don't want to go far to find it or wait in line when I get there or pay much for it."

The **expressive** service provider is providing specifically what the consumer wants to consume, similar to the specialty good category characteristics. The consumer has allocated the evening to drive several miles for a sensual dining experience rather than a quick, inexpensive hamburger. Part of the perceived total service package provided includes comfortable atmosphere, decor, wine, and perhaps a little music along with that delicious hour-and-a-half meal.

Q1-13 Is your service instrumental or expressive?

## Life Cycle Stage

Another way to zero in on the relationship between your product or service and its target market is to determine which stage in the industry life cycle your product or service is at.

1.  **Introduction/Growth Stage.** If a product or service catches on, it may enter a period of rapid growth lasting several months or even years. Many firms may enter the industry during the period of expanding demand. Sales volume grows at an increasing rate, and profits in the industry rise sharply. Rival firms with their additional promotional efforts may actually enlarge the total market. For example, Apple Computer's initiation of the personal computer revolution has prompted over 400 hardware and software manufacturers to enter the arena.

2. **Maturity Stage.** Eventually, the level of market acceptance and sales volume reach a peak. Overall sales revenue may continue to rise somewhat, but the rate of increase falls off because expenses for promotion become heavy, price cutting may occur, and consumers are pressured into brand loyalty through repeat advertising. Firms that cannot keep up the pace drop out of the market or are acquired by other firms—often their competitors. Large firms begin to dominate the industry. For example, the personal computer arena, two of the industry leaders that had tremendous success in the early 1980s—Atari and Osborne—faced declining demand for their particular brand and had personnel layoffs in 1983. Products in this stage of the life cycle include automobiles and electric hair dryers.

3. **Saturation Stage.** When all the consumers who can or will use the product or service are already buying it, the market is relatively saturated. Sales volume and profit in the industry begin to fall. Marginal firms have left the market, and the number of competitors stabilizes. The firm's promotion strategies concentrate on enlarging the total market. Examples include the cosmetics industry, the small restaurant industry in San Francisco, and the relatively saturated market for color television sets—at least one in nearly every home in the United States.

4. **Decline Stage.** Demand for the product or service falls at an increasing rate at the end of the life cycle. Promotion is curtailed and becomes highly selective, and prices are cut to stimulate sales. More and more rivals drop out of the market. New products or services are developed to take the place of those that are now obsolete. Examples are all the latest summer fashions that go on sale for half price in July, black-and-white televisions, and slide rules.

The stage in the life cycle of a product or service will affect the approach to advertising, or communicating awareness to the target market. For instance, if you are introducing a product or service that is totally new to the marketplace, advertising will be needed just to educate your chosen target group about the product or service. Rather than taking the marketing strategy of finding a need and filling it you would have to approach your target market to create demand.

### Example: Educating Parents

> After years of education and less than satisfying work situations, John decided to become an entrepreneur by selling his own unique service. He targeted his market and defined it as "parents of college-bound students." His service is to provide educational and career counseling to junior and senior high school students. Competition? "None to speak of," he says. There are certain problems involved in introducing such a totally new service. His only competition is school advisors and parents. He has to educate parents that his service even exists, since it's "not something people run to the *Yellow Pages* to find." If successful, this innovative service will eventually attract competition from others, and will then progress into the next stage of growth. It may also go through many changes in price, packaging, and promotional strategy in the process.

The total length of the life cycle and the length of each of the stages vary considerably. A new clothing fashion may have a life span of one year with an introductory/growth stage of two months. But the automobile industry has been in the maturity stage for at least forty years. In any case, your firm's total market environment—including economic, technological, social and competitive factors—is constantly changing. When markets change, prices and promotion strategies must change accordingly. Customers' acceptance of a product or service also changes over time. Therefore, you will find it necessary to adjust to these perceived changes, focusing on optimizing a sales strategy given the change in market conditions.

---

Q1-14 My product or service is in which stage?
 __ Introduction/Growth Stage      __ Maturity Stage

 __ Saturation Stage               __ Decline Stage

---

# Chapter 2 Target Market Research

Since this book takes a market-centered approach, it is important to remember that as an entrepreneur your business exists to satisfy customers' perceived needs—both tangible and intangible—and make a profit as your reward for successful marketing. Marketing strategy is based on determining the needs and wants of various target market segments (buyer or user groups with similar needs, characteristics, and buying habits) and satisfying these needs with an appropriate mix of goods and services. It is essential to obtain as much information as possible about the buyer groups most likely to benefit from your product or service before launching a marketing campaign.

Research concentrates on gaining relevant information about your current or potential customers, their buying habits and special benefits they're seeking in your product or service.

Marketing research information can be used to help clarify the following:

o    **Differential Advantage.** What is your niche? What distinguishes your products and services from other competitors? Good marketing strategy involves utilizing what's special about you—your differential—in attracting customers. By segmenting your customers into groups with similar characteristics (and knowing the buying characteristics of different segments) you can determine your differential advantage compared with the competition and make better informed marketing decisions regarding image, packaging, and media selection. This topic is the subject of this chapter.

o    **Marketing Plan.** What is the best way to reach that group of consumers with those certain characteristics? How many potential customers are in that group? How will you best tell them about your product or service? What is your competition doing? How will you get certain customers to buy from you rather than the competition?

With a good understanding of target markets and the competition you will be able to make better decisions regarding plans for advertising—how, where, and what should be advertised and which media best reach prospective customers or clients. Those topics are covered in later chapters.

## Finding Your Strong Points

Consider the benefits or strengths of businesses that help attract target customer groups:

o    The personal relationship with the owner or employees is a major repeat drawing item for the local lunchery or deli, the neighborhood tavern, the local service station, the local bakery, the manufacturer's representative, the wholesaler you have been dealing with for several years.

o    Some services are bought based on loyalty and word-of-mouth recommendations, for example, remodeling services, interior decorating, or landscaping.

o    A particular group may support others with similar characteristics; for example, women business owners support women-owned businesses, small business owners support small business suppliers or fellow memebers of a local Chamber of Commerce.

o    Customers desire special services like grocery shopping, housesitting, lawn mowing, free delivery.

o    Products may be offered at lower cost or better quality than larger stores can offer, such as co-op membership grocery stores, or catalog stores.

Now list the special features of your product or service which may help differentiate it in the marketplace by filling in Worksheet 2.

## Worksheet 2 Special Features of Your Product or Service

### (Check the features that apply)

_ **EXPERIENCE** (as a salesperson, accountant, manager, plumber, engineer, artist)

_ **PERSONALITY ORIENTATION** (outgoing/sales, internal/research and planning, machinery/physical results)

_ **SINCERITY** (the striving to satisfy your customers)

_ **REPUTATION** (recognition for a specific capability, such as solving electronics problems, manufacturing, or insurance requirements problems)

_ **WIDE ACQUAINTANCESHIP** (recognized as a community leader, know many people in your community or in a specific industry)

_ **LARGE FOLLOWING** (many people think you an expert in a specific field)

_ **LOCATION** (downtown, near a bus line, in a local shopping center or business area)

_ **CONVENIENT** (on the route to many activities, home service, open evenings)

_ **CREDIT** (30-day open account, company or bank charge cards, or financing plan)

_ **DELIVERY SERVICE** (daily pickup and delivery, delivery when repaired)

_ **FAST SERVICE** (in by 10, out by 4; one-hour fast photo)

_ **ECONOMICAL** (low prices, discounted merchandise, quantity discounts)

_ **QUALITY** (the best, made to last)

_ **EASY-PAY PLAN** (bank or finance company plan, usually higher-priced items)

_ **GUARANTEES** (180-day unconditional guaranteed service, parts replacement)

_ **DIVERSE ARRAY OF PRODUCTS OR SERVICES** (one-stop shopping or service)

_ **HIGHER QUALITY OF LIFE** (more leisure, less bother, greater comfort)

_ **SOCIAL CONTRIBUTOR** (train handicapped or unemployed, one dollar of every sale goes toward specific cause)

_ **ONE-OF-A-KIND OFFER** (first to offer, exclusive, only outlet available)

_ **SPECIAL MARKETS** (queen or king-sized, big and tall, petite)

_ **WARRANTIES AND RETURN POLICY** (return any merchandise if not satisfied, only pay for the pictures you want)

\_ LIGHTWEIGHT (material breathes, fewer calories, even a child can lift)

\_ HEAVYWEIGHT (rugged, outlasts the rest, exceeds warranty requirements)

\_ COMPACT (takes up little space, fits under airline seats, fits in purse)

\_ LARGE (does the big jobs, more trunk space, heavy-duty)

\_ NATURAL (no preservatives, all natural ingredients, natural fibers)

\_ IMPORTED (the world's finest, found nowhere else, exotic)

\_ HIGH RESALE VALUE (always in demand, always get your money's worth)

\_ GOOD INVESTMENT (houses, paintings, classic autos, income-producing)

\_ IN VOGUE (hottest new fashion, latest video game)

\_ PERSONAL TOUCH (your personal banker, agent or salesperson knows you by name)

\_ ADDS VALUE TO YOUR INVESTMENT (landscaping, solar heating, insulation)

\_ REMOVES EMBARRASSMENT (covers the gray, deodorizes, removes wrinkles)

\_ FUTURISTIC (ultra modern, the latest in automated equipment)

\_ SHOWS CLASS (good taste, high class restaurant or boutique, appeals to stars)

\_ INCREASES SEX APPEAL (appear more youthful, sexy taste or smell, sensual)

\_ TRADING STAMPS (special coupon offers, cumulative buying effect free)

\_ CONTESTS (sweepstakes prizes galore, don't have to buy to win, enter often)

\_ AVAILABILITY OF SPECIAL ITEMS (racing forms, lottery tickets, licenses)

\_ DEPOSIT (for recycling, bottle returns, gas cans available)

\_ EXPRESS SERVICE (automated checkout lanes, teller machines, curbside service)

\_ LAYAWAY PLAN (no interest charged, incentive to buy now)

\_ FREE SERVICES INCLUDED (babysitting, gift wrapping)

\_ FREE LESSONS (at your home or in our store, on-site training classes)

\_ PARKING (free if validated with purchase, covered garage nearby, valet service)

\_ INSTALLATION (included with purchase of carpet, computer, sprinkler system)

_ FREE TRIAL OFFER (money back if not satisfied, free samples)

_ MAIL ORDER SERVICES (save the sales commission)

_ SHIP ANYWHERE FREE (buy on vacation, receive it when you arrive home)

_ BRIDAL REGISTRY (home purchase items)

_ OTHER SPECIAL FEATURES

---

Now summarize what differential advantages can distinguish your product or service in the marketplace.

## Determining Your Market Segments

Clarifying specific marketing segments is a critical step in overcoming a rather common problem new small business owners are faced with—achieving a clear market position. The small business owner must understand why people purchase a specific product or service—i.e., what is the product or service's appeal? Is it courtesy, the personal touch, pleasure, quality, fun, escape, efficiency, competency, ease of credit terms, the price, location, prestige, status, safety, durability, guarantee or refund policy?

There is a tendency for many small businesses to set up shop and take any customer—offer any product or service in order to get business. Usually this is not a useful or profitable strategy, as the following examples will demonstrate.

### Example: "With a weld weld here and a weld weld there..."

Joe was a mobile welder who left his calling cards all over the state of Washington, although he lived in Seattle. He wanted all the business he could obtain, so his schedule was determined by geographic response to his business card. An analysis of his billing indicated the following schedule:

| | |
|---|---|
| Monday | 9-10 a.m. in Yakima (two hours East of Seattle) 3-4 p.m. in Richland (another two hour drive beyond Yakima, resulting in a four hour return trip to Seattle) |
| Tuesday | 12-3 p.m. in Bellingham (two hours north of Seattle) 5-7 p.m. in Seattle |
| Wednesday | 10-11 a.m. in Bellingham 2-7 p.m. in Seattle |
| Thursday and Friday | Open time for incoming calls (throughout the state) |

Joe had a shotgun marketing approach. To maintain a locally competitive price for his service he refused to charge travel time or expenses. Joe was rapidly going broke without more specific geographic targeting for his unique service.

Defining the target market is more an art than a science, but appropriate adjustments can usually be made. Had Joe been more specific in targeting a service area, he might have spent money and time to secure local business, and with success expanded (with more mobile units) into other areas of the state. By not defining his market, he made inefficient use of his time and resources. By not recognizing and advertising his uniqueness, he overlooked his differential advantage.

**Example: "We will build it, destroy it, move it, marry it..."**

Jayne was a superb typist and office manager who opened her own one-person business in a large downtown office building. She advertised the following services on the front page of her brochure:

*Office Management: Typing by the page, collating, direct mail services, office layout consultant, office space coordinator, photocopying, binding, training for interviewing, collection, EEOC advising, word processing.*

And that was a sampling. She would even housesit.

Jayne should have specialized her services rather than try to be all things to all people. At the time all indications were that word processing would be her best specialty, since it was new and offered her a competitive advantage. However, she could not stand the thought of not going after the other needs she could meet. She did not take time to check out her competition to determine who might already be providing some of the many services she was competent enough to offer.

**Example: "Office emporium and roadside attraction"**

Jack Clark had an office supplies and furnishings shop located in a commercial office complex in a metropolitan shopping area. He was attempting to create an image by calling his shop "Clark Designs," but other than the name, neither the company image nor his target market was obvious. He wanted to serve the professional offices upstairs... and there were those noontime shoppers who worked in the building who would be going to lunch and might stroll by... and those well-heeled homemakers on the East side who wanted upper-class home furnishings... there was a significant group who shopped from out North... and a tour outfit that just happened to unload at his doorstep.

He had tourist items in the windows-not effectively using the window display for his best target group, the professional offices upstairs. The well-healed homemaker was turned off by the "tourist stuff." The professional office furniture buyers were not eager to mingle with casual shoppers. Basically his location was excellent—if he concentrated on one specific target group and cut out his broad image advertising. Because he did not want a single possible buyer to miss seeing his name, image advertising was wasted.

**Example: "Frames on wheels?"**

A frame-it-yourself shop was barely making a profit, and therefore decided to diversify. It was a shop catering to a middle-aged, middle-income, mostly female target group. The shop owners (a husband-and-wife team) also sold prepared frames and gave framing lessons. They decided to start selling truck licenses to get some additional income—an apparent opportunity.

A visitor to their shop would notice well-framed, high-quality art works for sale, displayed in the reception area in front of a self-framing counter. A trucker might walk in to buy a license from the husband while the wife continued teaching her framing class at the front working counter.

Success? The husband-owner was delighted to sell truck licenses because he much preferred dealing with truckers. Unfortunately, the diversification did not enhance the frame business. The owners sold the business rather than put more effort into the target market the business was already set up to serve. The current owners do not sell truck licenses, and the frame business appears to be healthier, due to a closer tie-in with art and photography courses at nearby schools and colleges. The owners of the shop are focusing their efforts on fulfilling the needs of a specific target group.

By comparison, the following businesses provide more definitive statements describing the specific market segments they serve.

### Example: Oasis Press

Oasis Press in Milpitas, California, "a publisher of innovative aids for small business," describes itself with the following statement, from its promotional literature.

"Oasis Press develops and markets innovative communications aids for small business. We see ourselves as facilitating communication, whether communication of problem solving methods from the expert to the business person, or communication between the business person and his or her various constituencies. We draw upon our considerable entrepreneurial experience, our empathy with the small business person, a continual "ear to the ground" with a network of other business people, and a carefully fostered sensitivity to social change, as well as conventional marketing research, to focus on finding unmet communication needs, and on developing the right new product to meet those needs. We concentrate on innovation, on small market niches, and low overhead production. We promote and distribute in a variety of traditional and non-traditional channels to reach our distinct target audience, but stress direct mail, office supply stores, and mass market book stores."

### Example: Pacific Electronics

"Pacific Electronics specializes in prototyping, testing, and producing high-technology printed circuit board assemblies for the medical, telecommunications and commercial electronics industries.

- o  Quality manufacturing techniques
- o  Convenience and cost savings
- o  Service
- o  Consulting services

"With over 25 years of industry experience, we assemble the boards, wire harnesses, and wire wrap. From schematics, we develop reliable breadboards and customized testers while guiding the board from prototype to production.

"We are capable of producing a high volume of different electronic and mechanical assemblies and provide skilled hand soldering for special applications. We offer short-run, quick-turnaround services and are experienced in reworking existing assemblies and cables.

"Our normal quality of work standards are those required by the rigorous demands of the health-service industry. However, we will meet any assembly requirement."

The following example presents relevant marketing questions and gives sample responses intended to help analyze various target market segments and develop profiles of typical customer groups. A worksheet follows to assist you in answering these questions for your product or service.

### Example: A Shoe Repair Business

One prospective small business entrepreneur wanted to buy a shoe repair business. He did some research of the market to help him see the business from the market's point of view. He found in broad terms that the market for this shoe repair shop is the community in which it is located. For the most part, people do not travel far from their homes or places of business for shoe repair services. Generally, there are two forms of competition: other repair shops and new shoes.

The following questions are useful in identifying specific target groups, their characteristics, and their buying habits.

Q2-1   What **benefits** is the customer seeking?

o   Repair and restyling of shoes and related leather goods
o   Orthopedic corrections
o   Greater comfort (stretching of shoes, extra notch in belt)
o   Related products (polishes, shoelaces)

Q2-2   What **factors** influence demand?

o   Seasons—wet weather and winter make people more aware of their shoes
o   Prices of new items
o   Perception of repairability: if a potential customer thinks an item can't be repaired, it probably won't be brought in, but if the customer is aware that a service such as dyeing can be performed, it is more likely to be requested

Q2-3   What **functions** does the product or service perform for the customer?

o   Extends the life of favorite items
o   Saves money if item can be repaired for less than the cost to replace it
o   Satisfies personal needs by restyling to customer's satisfaction
o   Provides comfort with necessary corrections

Q2-4   What are important **buying criteria?**

o   Price in relation to seeking and purchasing replacement items
o   Quality of work; past experience with shop
o   Knowing what services are available

Q2-5   What is the **basis of comparison** with other products?

o   Price and style of new items
o   Quality of work
o   Convenient location
o   Knowledge of what can be accomplished

Q2-6   What **risks** does the customer **perceive?**

o   Might spend a lot and not get satisfactory job
o   Item might be damaged or lost
o   Worries about what repair person thinks of customer's particular problem

Q2-7   What services do customers expect?

o   Expect items to be repaired and as close to "new" looking as possible
o   Individual attention
o   Completion of work in reasonable amount of time (even "while-you-wait" service), expect items to be ready when promised

Q2-8   How do customers decide to **buy?**

o   Locate or decide on a shop; visit with items to be repaired; ask if work can be done and at what price; leave work; pickup as arranged and pay

Q2-9   How long does the **buying process last?**

o   Varies: some people shop for this service, while others use the nearest shop, like a dry cleaner in a local shopping area

Q2-10  How much are customers **willing to spend?**

    o   Depends on what it would cost relative to buying new items
    o   Often depends on how much longer they think items will last
    o   Depends on what it will look like when repaired

Q2-11  **How much** do they buy? How **frequently?**

    o   Typical customer brings in one or two items per family member two or three times a year

Q2-12  **When** is the **decision made** to buy?

    o   Varies; usually at the time the problem is noticed
    o   Special occasions or unusual situations
    o   Direct mail coupon or local advertisement initiates action

Q2-13  Where do customers **seek information** about the product or service?

    o   Usually in the *Yellow Pages,* or they are already aware of the shop in their neighborhood or near their place of work

    o   They may ask neighbors or local merchants

Q2-14  What kinds of locations attract customers to buy the product or service?

    o   Typically at repair shop or sometimes from repair shop located in a department store

Q2-15  Why do customers **choose one brand** or service outlet over another?

    o   Convenient location
    o   Favorable experience with work
    o   Bad experience at another shop
    o   Reputation for specializing in particular service, such as orthopedics

Q2-16  Who are the **occupants of segments** identified by previous questions?

    o   People living or working in vicinity of shop
    o   People requiring a specialized service provided by the shop

Now, fill in the following market segment worksheet for your business.

**Worksheet 3 Target Market Analysis Questionnaire**

1. What benefits does the product or service offer the consumer? Who can use it? What benefits is the consumer seeking? (Q2-1)

2. What factors influence demand? (Is demand sensitive to general economic condition? Other prices of similar item?) (Q2-2)

3. What function does the product or service perform? (Q2-3)

4. What are important buying criteria? (Q2-4)

5. What is the basis of comparison with other products or services? (Q2-5)

6. What risks does the customer perceive in the purchase? (Q2-6)

7. What services do the customers expect? (Q2-7)

8. How do customers decide to buy? (Q2-8)

9. How long does the buying process last? (Q2-9)

10. How much are customers willing to spend? (Q2-10)

11. How much do they buy? How frequently? (Q2-11)

12. When is the decision made to buy? (Q2-12)

13. Where do customers seek information about the product or service? (Q2-13)

14. Where do you now sell (or plan to sell) the product or service? (Q2-14)

15. Why do customers choose one brand or service over another? (Q2-15)

16. Define the typical occupants of your various target market segments, as identified by responses to previous questions (Who makes up your market segments? What are their needs? What are they really buying? How is the buying process influenced?) (Q2-16)

## Market Research

If you want to learn more about your target groups, market research can be conducted in many ways. Major ways that we will discuss are

o Reading materials relating to your particular industry
o Direct observation
o Performing controlled experiments
o Utilizing focus groups

The use of controlled experiments or focus groups will also help zero in on target market segments. Utilizing surveys, whether oral or written, is a particularly valuable way of pinpointing product characteristics or consumer preferences which you may not be aware of.

In advance of launching a marketing campaign, there are low-cost resources that can help you determine the feasibility of succeeding in the market.

Many daily and weekly newspapers conduct ongoing market research. They often provide the information for their metropolitan area of interest by census tract. They may also be able to provide maps showing geographic concentration of various business activities such as shopping centers, supermarkets, and recreational areas. By combining information about demographic characteristics (such as age, sex, marital status, average household earnings, etc.) with business activity information, you should be able to create a map to estimate the demand characteristics for your product or service.

Many daily newspapers have a weekly special geographical section like "North End Business Review." Neighborhood areas may have their own weekly newspaper or shoppers' tabloid. If you are intending to locate in its area of coverage, the newspaper should be eager to share its research statistics with you as a potential advertiser.

Q2-17 Daily or weekly newspapers to check with include:

Neighborhood newspapers include:

University or public libraries are some of the best places to start a feasibility study for a majority of business products or services. They contain a plethora of information about business trends, industry trends, specific studies published by consumer research groups, marketing surveys, and a copy of valuable information furnished through other sources discussed below. Key publications that assist with your marketing research include: *Standard and Poor's Industry Surveys, Encyclopedia of Associations, Key Business Ratios, Census of Population, Census of Business, The Survey of Buying Power, Annual Statement Studies,* and the various publications published by the U.S. Small Business Administration (SBA).

> Q2-18 Local public or university libraries include:

Government publications, particularly those of the U.S. Department of Commerce and the Small Business Administration, are extremely valuable sources of information about your target market characteristics. The Department of Commerce can provide census data and industry-by-industry sales statistics. The Department of *Commerce's Franchise Company Data* contains a wealth of information about franchises such as capital required, financial management, and training assistance. The SBA offers valuable services to the business entrepreneur. You can get practical marketing information from many of the aids they have published. They also conduct monthly seminars on a broad range of small business topics. Their services and publications are either free or at very low cost.

Free consulting is also available through the SBA's SCORE group (Service Corps of Retired Executives) and ACE (Active Corps of Executives). Contact your nearest SBA office to set up an appointment. The corps can also help you do business with the federal government, if it happens to be one of your target groups. Send or call for an SBA free publication list.

> Q2-19 Telephone number of closest SBA or SCORE office is:

Banks are a natural source of information regarding the local business climate and newcomers to your marketplace. They may also have a research and statistics department which could prove helpful. Convincing a loan officer who handles small business accounts that you are a potential business customer should also net you much relevant information.

> Q2-20 My bank and the loan officer I am dealing with are:

Joining your local Chamber of Commerce is one of the best networking techniques for the small business person, since its membership is composed of other entrepreneurs in your local community. Many chambers have monthly publications of general business interest, as well as monthly meetings to share successes and problems of being a small business owner or manager.

> **Q2-21** Telephone number of the local Chamber of Commerce is:

Of the over 5000 trade associations that exist in the United States, one is very likely to be aligned with your specific product or service. Check in the *Directory* or *Encyclopedia of Associations* at the local library for the address of the closest associations connected with your business, then visit them or write to obtain relevant information such as industry sales, marketing surveys, and forecasts.

> **Q2-22** The relevant trade association for my business is
>
> Address
>
> Telephone
>
> Contact person

Businesses in related services or product lines will always be helpful to talk to. Suppliers to retail businesses, for example, are often a good source of information on local pricing policies, trends within product lines, new packaging ideas, and the latest technological advances. Of course, talking to your perceived competitors, becoming aware of their advertising, wandering through their stores or service outlets, and getting to know whom they choose for a lawyer and accountant will serve you well in attempting to target your market to its best differential advantage.

> **Q2-23** I can learn from businesses in related services or product lines in the following ways:

## Research Survey Techniques

The above-mentioned sources of information can be highly useful in segmenting a target market and clarifying the potential demand for your product or service. These sources, however, do not involve interactive marketing research, which is more expensive—and often more interesting and direct. The following examples of research survey techniques give an idea of direct ways to gather relevant information about the demographics of the target group, such as economic status and spending habits, as well as psychological influences that should be considered.

The nature of the questions asked, experiments undertaken, or observations made will depend entirely on what you want to know about target groups of customers. Through direct questions about the needs of target customers and their degree of satisfaction with your product or service in comparison with competitors, you will get a better grasp of the overall market position and marketing strategy. Market research surveys can be very flexible in the way they help gather information. Once a questionnaire is assembled, several options for conducting your research become available.

**Observation.** A very simple direct approach to research is to simply go to the location of the intended business (or to a competitor's business) and observe buyer characteristics such as age, style of dress, method of transportation, and any other relevant factors. For example, a woman we know who was interested in buying an ice cream franchise and locating in Napa, California spent one day of every weekend for four months casually standing on different street corners counting the number of people who walked by. She was able to determine the best apparent location for her new business, as well as to familiarize herself with potential customers and her business environment. Other ways of observing both target customers and competition involve:

o Reading the *Yellow Pages* of the phone book under the headings related to your product or service

o Observing the local competitor's approaches to selling their products or services at their place of business

o Counting the cars or pedestrians that go by the anticipated location at different times of the day and week.

o Observing, if the anticipated location is on the sunny side of the street (more attractive window shopping) and on the "going home" side of the street (impulse shopping on the way home from work or school).

Q2-24 What kinds of information could you find by the observation method?

How can the information be used?

**Controlled experiments.** This approach is particularly useful in determining whether to add a new product or service to your current business. Examples include pricing a new product differently at different store locations, having a 2-for-1 sale, or utilizing sample handouts—at a grocery store, for instance—and recording the number of people who respond by purchasing the new item.

Q2-25 How might you utilize a controlled experiment?

**Focus group interviews.** This research approach has gained considerable attention in recent years, and has been especially instructive to entrepreneurs introducing new products or services into the marketplace. In focus group interviews, eight to ten people are gathered by the researchers to discuss a particular new product or service while the interview is being taped.

For example, one college dormitory group was asked to try out a new haircutting device that had an attachment to vacuum the hair while the device was cutting. The product looked similar to a hair dryer. The item was shown, described in terms of product features and advantages to the user, and then demonstrated. The interviewer asked the group to brainstorm why they might buy the product— or why they would not. Whom did they feel would be the best target customers for this device? What price would be reasonable for the product?

This process was repeated with a group of married people in their twenties and early thirties with young children. The only cost was for dessert. The factor that surfaced as a concern for this group was the fear of making a mistake, especially on their children. The entrepreneur learned that he would have to figure out some way to alleviate the fear-of-mistakes factor or else change his intended target market.

Q2-26 What questions might be asked if you were to utilize a focus
group interview?

1.

2.

3.

4.

5.

6.

**Direct mail.** You can purchase mailing lists, containing names of individuals that
might be in your target market, and send them your survey, asking them to
kindly fill it out and return it. You can send it to past customers, target groups
in the telephone book, or a totally random group of people obtained from a
mailing list. As questionnaires are returned, the task becomes one of tabulating
the results to obtain useful information about potential customers.

Q2-27 Which mailing lists would be useful?

**Personal interviews.** These can be conducted with questionnaires in hand at the
location of the business involved. This is a particularly useful technique because
you can develop eye contact and glean information about potential customers
through observation as well as by tabulating questionnaire results.

Q2-28 Will personal interviews be useful and easy to obtain?
What customer reactions or characteristics will you look for?

**Telephone interviews.** This is one of the most frequently used methods of gather-
ing market research information. Using a standardized format, many interviews
can be conducted in a relatively short period of time. Using a list of current
customers or customers with the same phone prefix is customary. Using voice-
activated computers is also becoming an efficient telephone interview technique.

Q2-29 What telephone interviewing techniques might be useful?
Who would make the phone calls?

Utilizing a combination of survey techniques can definitely help identify a particular target market, a competitor's product or service mix, and any needs still unmet or unsatisfied by what exists in the marketplace.

Q2-30 List the information you would particularly like to know about

Your competition

Your competitors' customers

Your own customers

Q2-31 Summarize the information sources to be utilized in your marketing research.

Q2-32 Which survey research techniques do you think will be most useful?

Why?

## Market Research Survey Questionnaires

Whether launching a new product or service into the marketplace, adding a new one, or reviewing your target group's satisfaction with your current offering, research survey questionnaires can be extremely useful. As mentioned earlier, the particular questions asked should be relevant to whatever you need to know. The following sample questionnaire* indicates some general types of questions you may be interested in when developing a survey instrument. Usually a questionnaire is prefaced with a statement on its purpose and intended use, for example: "This is an independent survey to help us better serve our customers. We will appreciate your taking a moment to fill it out and return it to us."

## Channels of Distribution

The whole marketing process involves producing, pricing, distributing, and promoting goods and services to existing and potential customers at a profit. Decisions regarding which channels of distribution to utilize are important to assure the greatest amount of profitable accessibility to the customer. Typical channels of distribution are shown below:

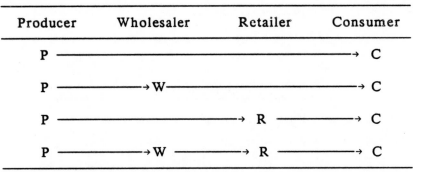

| Producer | Wholesaler | Retailer | Consumer |
|----------|-----------|----------|----------|
| P ————————————————————————→ C | | | |
| P ——————→ W————————————→ C | | | |
| P ————————————————→ R ————→ C | | | |
| P ——————→ W ——→ R ————→ C | | | |

The business entrepreneur (producer or service provider) must match the ability to produce and supply goods and services with the needs and demands of the various market segments or target groups.

Given the special nature of your product or service, selecting an appropriate distribution system becomes part of your overall marketing plan and can affect other marketing decisions such as business location, pricing strategy, advertising, and sales promotion. For instance, the nature of perishable goods requires either shorter supply channels or utilization of large-volume, widespread wholesalers to get perishables to the consumer. Almost all professional services go from producer/professional direct to consumer, unless their labor is subcontracted through a retail organization such as a referral agency.

*Adapted from *Pleasing Your Boss—the Customer* by Dwayne Laws, SBA Small Marketers Aids Number 114, Washington, D.C. A more sophisticated questionnaire is presented in Appendix B.

## SURVEY QUESTIONS

1. When do you prefer to shop? ____ a.m. to ____ p.m.

2. If you like evening shopping, which nights of the week do you prefer?

   Monday __ Tuesday __ Wednesday __ Thursday __
   Friday __ Saturday __ Sunday __

3. How do you prefer to pay?
   cash __ credit __ charge card __

4. What quality of merchandise do you usually buy?
   high __ moderate __ low __

5. What type of store do you prefer to shop in?
   conventional service oriented __ discount __ high fashion __

6. How do you take care of various problems you may have with your purchases?
   fix it myself __ return it to store __ outside repair __

7. Who does most of the buying in your family?
   male __ female __ children __

8. What is your average annual family income?
   under $10,000 __ $10,000 to $30,000 __ over $30,000 __

9. What is the age of your major family purchaser? _____

10. Which newspapers do you most often read?

    Which sections?

11. Which magazines do you enjoy reading?

12. Which radio stations do you listen to?

    What hours do you generally listen?

13. Which television programs do you usually watch during the week?

14. Any comments you wish to make?

   **Thank you for your cooperation.**

Other things being equal, the more standardized the product and the lower the unit value, the longer the channel of distribution. Many producers of consumer goods use the P-W-R-C channel because it enables a small company with a limited line of products to utilize the promotional resources and buyer networks provided by large wholesalers with broad market access. While this approach to product distribution gives the lowest cost to the manufacturer or service provider (because others take over the distribution and promotion), it also requires relinquishing control when title of the goods passes to wholesaler and then retailer.

Several different channels may be used. Some items such as soap products may be distributed through the third channel of grocery wholesalers to food stores to consumers. They may also utilize the second channel with the manufacturer selling to large retail chains and motels. Amway and Avon move their products from producer to sales people to consumer. L.L. Bean may offer goods directly by mail order to the consumer; Eddie Bauer has retail stores as well as mail-order catalogs.

A jewelry designer may have a studio, where customers can buy direct, as well as utilize large retail department stores throughout the United States (and overseas) to sell merchandise. The incentive for a customer to buy direct from the producer is generated by both the opportunity to meet the artist and the opportunity to buy at a discount.

---

Q2-33 Describe the major channels of distribution you plan to utilize.

---

Q2-34 Describe the channels of distribution used by your competitors.

---

Q2-35 How might your distribution strategy affect sales? Competition?

## Determining an Appropriate Business Location

Along with determining a distribution strategy, the business entrepreneur also needs to determine an appropriate location. While distribution strategy is affected by the nature of the goods and services, location strategy is more closely related to customer demands, buying habits, and projected product or service image. It has often been said that the major selling points in the real estate service industry consist of "location, location, and location." If you have a retail outlet, choose a location that is consistent with the image you want. If you want to portray convenience, choosing a location that's difficult to find will affect how you advertise it. If you are manufacturing a new product, you may want to find a location that is close to your suppliers. If you are providing a service, such as accounting or law, you may want a location that gives the image of prestige. If you are in the mail-order business, your location should be near a delivery route or central post office where mail can easily reach you.

Consider the following factors in site selection:

o   The selection of a particular geographic area such as a city;

o   The selection of a district within that geographic area—i.e., a suburban shopping center or the downtown business district; and

o   The selection of a particular site within your chosen district.

The term site selection generally refers to the overall strategy of finding the most suitable location to serve your target market. Several factors about site location should be kept in mind when determining this element of your marketing strategy:

o   While having a good location doesn't guarantee marketing success, it certainly is a major element in retailing to mass markets and in providing many services such as cleaning, banking, and shoe repair.

o   Having a poor location and a high-quality product is not conducive to developing a positive image. More advertising dollars will be needed to help communicate awareness of a product or service, since target customers will be less likely to frequent a bad location.

o   Because a marketing environment constantly changes, as do customer's needs, be aware of other locations which could serve as well. For instance, when it comes time to renew the lease, consider whether the location and its associated costs are justified. Consider the element of location as a trade-off with other factors of your marketing mix.

o   If you provide a service, will customers be coming to you, or will you be going to them? Most retail service outlets have customers coming to their location, so it needs to be compatible with the target customers' needs: convenience, parking, and shopping. If you are a free-lance photographer, management consultant, or tree-trimming service, you will travel to your clientele, so office location will be of less significance in helping achieve a clear market position.

o   Basic market factors as well as budget considerations should determine the business location. If the target market is suburban housewives, it may be more beneficial to locate the business in a regional shopping area. If the target group is the teenage video game market, locate the product in local neighborhood sites to make the product accessible. A used car dealership may find it desirable to locate next to a new automobile showroom. In any case, finding a suitable location and making your product or service accessible to the target market is essential in achieving marketing success.

---

**Q2-36 Describe the characteristics and advantages of your chosen (or ideal) business location.**

---

**Q2-37 What is the most distinguishing characteristic or feature of this location?**

**How can it best be utilized as part of your marketing strategy?**

---

Now that you have described your business location, summarize its advantages by utilizing the following worksheet. (It reflects your subjective evaluation of this important marketing tool.) You may want to review previous questions and worksheets (especially in this chapter) before rating your location.

## Worksheet 4 Business Location Evaluation

Rate each of the following location criteria.

| | Poor | Fair | Good | Excellent | |
|---|---|---|---|---|---|
| Does there appear to be much of a need for this product or service? | | | | | (Q2-1 to 4) |
| How centrally located is it to my major consumers? | | | | | (Q2-32 to 37) |
| Approximately how concentrated are potential consumers in my market area? | | | | | (Q2-17 to 24; 33 to 35) |
| The competitive environment is | | | | | (Worksheets 1-3; Q2-33 to 35) |
| The community's current level of ability to support my business is | | | | | (Worksheets 1-3) |
| The community's growth potential is | | | | | (Worksheets 1-3) |
| Availability of the major kinds of transportation my customers will use is | | | | | (Worksheets 1-3; (Q2-36, 37) |
| Parking facilities are | | | | | (Q2-36, 37) |
| The degree of consistency regarding demographics of the population with my needs (age, sex, education, income, occupation) is | | | | | (Q2-17 to 32) |
| The desirability of this location in relation to my supplier is | | | | | (Q2-33 to 35) |
| The availability and affordability of the type of employees are | | | | | (Q2-36, 37) |
| The flow of passers-by indicated is | | | | | (Q2-24, 28, 29, 30) |

| | Poor | Fair | Good | Excel-lent | |
|---|---|---|---|---|---|
| How important is the going-home side of the street to your business? | | | | | (Q2-24, 28, 29, 30) |
| The importance of your location in relation to the sunny side of the street is | | | | | (Q2-24, 28, 29, 30) |
| The attractiveness of my location to me in terms of living and working in this community is | | | | | (Worksheets 1-3) |

## Determining Your Differential Advantage

Once you have gathered information from all sources, you must summarize the results in a way that is meaningful for developing an overall marketing strategy and putting it into a marketing plan. By now you need to be familiar with the target market segments—the characteristics and buying habits of potential customer groups, the special features of your product or service, the competitive environment, and the most appropriate pricing, location, and distribution strategies. These differentiating features help identify your market advantage and can become critical elements in a successful marketing campaign.

When identifying and differentiating a new product or service to chosen market segments, what you are actually selling is a combination of the good or service itself and the various service features in the total purchase package. For example, purchasing a piano may include free delivery, free lessons, or a free tune-up. Purchasing furniture might include some interior decorator consulting, free delivery, or color counseling. One personal computer retail store includes free lessons. This method has proved to be a successful way of positioning itself in the volatile personal computer market. Knowing your particular product or service mix will help you identify your differential advantage in the marketplace.

Worksheet 5, Target Market Research Summary and Customer, Company, Competition Profile is designed to help summarize the relevant characteristics of the target market(s) and your product or service compared with competitors. Review all previous worksheets and questions and add or subtract characteristics which are most applicable to your particular business. When completed, this worksheet will represent a profile of your chosen target market segments and a summary of your differential advantage, a starting point from which to launch a marketing campaign.

**Worksheet 5 Target Market Research Summary**

The clearer the business description, the better guide your business will have in clarifying the products or services it provides, the markets it serves, and the best promotional strategy for success.

First describe your business by answering the following questions:

1. What are you selling? Give some examples (Q1-1 to 14, Worksheet 1)

2. What are you offering that is unique to you or that distinguishes your product or service from others? (Worksheets 1 - 3)

3. Who buys this product or service? Who are your market segments? (Q2-16)

4. Why are they buying it? What is it they are buying? (Worksheets 1 - 4)

5. How do you provide this product or service? (Q2-24 to 35)

6. The following are areas of differential competitive advantage for: (Q2-30 to 37)

    o My organization, product, or service.

    o My competitor's organization, product, or service.

Customer, Company, Competition Profile

Product or service description:

| Customer Characteristics (refer to Worksheets 1 to 4 and Chapter 2 examples) | My company | Competitor |
|---|---|---|
| 1. Age range | | |
| 2. Sex of buyer | | |
| 3. Education | | |
| 4. Income range | | |
| 5. Occupations | | |
| 6. Location of customers | | |
| 7. Lifestyle/marital status | | |
| 8. Culture/values | | |
| 9. Needs met | | |
| 10. Sources of transportation | | |
| 11. Other | | |
| 12. Major ways to pay (credit cards, etc.) | | |
| 13. Days, months, hours of business | | |
| 14. Media read | | |
| 15. Radio or TV stations | | |

| Product/Service/Co. (refer to Worksheets 1 to 4) | | |
|---|---|---|
| 1. Price | | |
| 2. Quality (Worksheet 2) | | |
| 3. Stage in life cycle of product (Q1-14) | | |
| 4. Design/styling (Worksheet 2) | | |
| 5. Services offered (Worksheet 2) | | |
| 6. Seasonal/cyclical patterns (Worksheet 3) | | |
| 7. Credit terms (Worksheet 3) | | |
| 8. Hours open (Worksheet 3) | | |
| 9. Location of business (Worksheet 3) | | |
| 10. Specific strengths (Q2-30 to 32) | | |
| 11. Specific weaknesses (Q2-30 to 32) | | |
| 12. Our product/service position (Worksheet 3) | | |
| 13. Media used to advertise | | |
| 14. Type of specialty (Worksheet 1) | | |
| 15. Major way sold (retail, mail, etc.) (Q2-33 to 35) | | |
| 16. Channels of distribution (producer-to-consumer, etc.) (Q2-33 to 35) | | |
| 17. Years in business | | |
| 18. Packaging of product or service (Worksheet 2) | | |

Finally, write a full business description showing your competitive advantages
(Refer to the market segment example in this chapter.)

# Chapter 3 Basic Pricing Formats

Selling price usually reflects three basic elements: the cost to you of the goods or services sold (labor and materials), also called direct cost, administrative and selling expenses (overhead), also called indirect cost, and profit. Other factors which will influence the pricing decision include the nature of the product or service, company policy, competition, business conditions, market strategy, and distribution methods. In general a markup approach to pricing is used.

> Selling Price = Purchase Cost + Markup

Initial markup (also referred to as gross margin) is the difference between selling price and purchase cost, and should be large enough to cover overhead expenses and still provide a satisfactory profit. In other words,

> Markup = Selling Price - Purchase Cost = Gross Margin

Markup or gross margin can be expressed either as a percentage of selling price or as a percentage of cost.

Most retailers and service businesses express markup as a percentage of selling price. For example, consider a toy shop owner who purchases a line of tricycles that cost $60 each. Her research shows that a 40% markup (as a percentage of retail price) will cover selling expenses and still provide a satisfactory profit. The formula used to help determine an appropriate selling price is:

$$\text{Selling Price} = \frac{\text{Purchase Cost}}{100\% \text{ markup on retail}} \times 100$$

$$= \frac{\$60}{(100 - 40)} \times 100 \quad \frac{\$60}{60} = \times 100$$

$$= \$1 \times 100 = \$100 \text{ (or probably \$99.95 for psychological reasons)}$$

If a retailer purchases mixers at $50 each and wants a 45% markup as a percent of retail, the retailer would price the item as follows:

$$\text{Selling Price} = \frac{\$50}{(100 - 45)} \times 100 = \frac{50}{55} \times 100 = \$90.91$$

You may want to actually price this item differently to meet customer buying psychology, e.g. $89.95 or even up to $99.95, which would allow a greater gross margin than 45%.

Businesses often use a standard markup that is very similar to what their competitors use for the same or a similar item. Their gross margin (markup) should cover direct and indirect expenses, yet provide a profit.

Appendix A presents a detailed procedure for getting retail prices.

Most businesses in the service industry usually provide a variety of specialized services. Every service provided should contribute toward overall profit and bear its share of expenses. This requires a bookkeeping system that keeps track of costs and operating expenses associated with each kind of service. Direct costs (labor, materials) and indirect ·costs (which vary with the services provided) are thereby allocated to each specific service.

In personal service establishments, some pricing is practically a given—guild pricing used by some beauty and barber shops, direct competitor's prices, limitations involved in franchise agreements. Other pricing practices will reflect a commonly accepted price for basic services by some of the major establishments. Most of the dry cleaners, for example, charge the same to clean a lady's plain dress. A man's business suit is also a commonly used standard. From basic standardized services a price schedule is set up for other standardized services. Special services usually are priced according to the amount of labor required and may be reflected in a flat service fee.

## The Multiplier Method of Pricing

When a service is provided for which there are no community standards, a method is used to allocate indirect costs called the multiplier method. Total sales is divided by annual labor costs. A new firm will do a fair amount of guessing and estimating to get this figure. Based on forecasts, let's assume a firm estimates that it will have annual sales of $50,000. It estimates that it will have total direct labor costs of $30,000.

Multiplier = Total Sales ÷ Annual Labor Costs

= $50,000 ÷ $30,000 = 1.67

This will hopefully cover indirect (overhead) costs and include a profit.

Next, to calculate the price to charge a client for a job which took three hours, the average worker's wage is multiplied times the number of hours which the job took and the indirect cost multiplier. For this example, assume the average wage is $15/hour.

3 hours x $15 x 1.67 = $75.15

This figure will reflect direct labor, indirect costs, and a profit.

To that amount ($75.15) is added the direct cost of materials utilized for that job (for example, $13.25). The total job price is billed to the client at $88.40 ($75.15 + $13.25).

## The Flat Rate Approach

Several types of businesses use flat rate pricing, using **price lists** suggested by the manufacturers or price-reporting services (such as those used by plumbing and heating contractors). Repair shops often rely on flat rates. The flat rate is calculated by figuring a standard time to do the job, multiplied by an average wage rate, times a multiplier (see the previous section). Those using this approach usually make the assumption that the **indirect cost-to-sales ratios are the same throughout a particular service industry.**

Rate = Standard job time x Average wage x Multiplier

Assume that a particular job took two hours, the average wage rate is $7.50, and the multiplier is 3.0, the job would cost

2 x $7.50 x 3 = $45

Sometimes the local wage rate is substituted for that in the published list.

Ultimately the price arrived at takes into account many other considerations in addition to cost plus profit margin.

## Professional Services and Consultants

Attorneys, architects, accountants, dentists, doctors, therapists, graphic and interior designers, and other professionals have several major approaches to pricing:

o  **By job**

standardized fee, used with set tasks like a simple divorce, incorporation, appendectomy, or filling.

or estimated:
   Average hours + Overhead + Materials + Profit

o  **By hour fee:**

determined by the going price in the community for having similar education, experience, and clientele

o  **By your required hourly income:**

Assume that there are 2000 hours per year that could be billed out to clients. Some professionals with support staffs consider 80% of those hours to be actually billable or sellable. In small businesses where the owner or manager is responsible for everything from marketing to office management to public relations, a figure of 40% to 50% is probably more realistic. At 1000 actual billable hours a year, then a professional service provider with relatively low overhead might determine an hourly fee as follows:

| | |
|---|---|
| Office rent | $400 x 12 months |
| Phone | 75 x 12 |
| Secretarial (half-time) | 400 x 12 |
| Supplies | 50 x 12 |
| Legal/accounting | 25 x 12 |
| Miscellaneous/mailing | 25 x 12 |
| Marketing | 50 x 12 |
| | $1025 x 12 = $12,300 |

Given the above costs of $12,300 per year with 1000 actual billable hours, $12.30 of each billable hour must go for overhead. You will need to determine a minimum gross annual salary which can cover these anticipated overhead expenses and provide a livable wage for your services. Assume you want to earn a draw or gross salary of $30,000 a year. That means you would need to bill clients at $30,000 ÷ 1000 hours = $30 (your labor) + $12.30 (office overhead) = $42.30/hour. If you are just starting out, there is a strong likelihood that it will be difficult to bill 1000 hours. So if it is possible to charge closer to $45 or $50 an hour, it would be more desirable in order to achieve your earnings goal. (You may also need to consider less income if the market conditions won't support a higher rate.)

A good many consultants look at the overhead estimates and decide to operate out of a home office or try to reduce rent and secretarial expenses significantly. Some bring in a partner or partners to begin with to share overhead expenses, since virtually the same overhead estimate may cover the overhead for two or three as well. Thus, the allocation per billable hour that must be included for overhead goes down. If the consultant in the example given adds one partner, each could bill now at $30 + $6.15 = $36.15 or probably $36 or $40 an hour (service pricing is usually rounded up). It may be necessary to try to bill more hours. When the business is new, it is usually necessary to spend more time getting clients or new business, which makes it difficult to secure the desired number of billable hours the first three or four years.

## Pricing for Small Manufacturers

The demand for some products is influenced a great deal by a change in price and can therefore be stimulated by advertising. Sales of ski equipment, fishing rods, and clothing at year-end can impact sales dramatically (high price sensitivity). However, if Nieman-Marcus marked its sable coats down from $43,000 to $41,000, or increased the price to $45,000, the quantity sold will probably not change much. Reducing the price of salt and advertising it as a great deal will probably have little impact on salt sales (low price sensitivity).

> **Q3-1** Describe how the sales of your product or service would be affected by an increase or decrease in price (price sensitivity).

In a manufacturing business, various market factors (i.e. the general economy, technological advances, competition, available resources) determine a ceiling price for a given product. Pricing your product above what the market will bear will greatly diminish sales. Given this upper pricing limit, how does the small manufacturer price products to cover costs, yet obtain a desirable profit?

In essence, manufacturers must remain cognizant of their **floor price**—that bottom line price which will cover costs and provide a reasonable profit. They can then determine a **relevant price range** which covers "floor costs" and stays below the ceiling price.

The approach taken to floor pricing manufactured items depends upon maintaining accurate and current cost data (work with your accountant in determining specific relevant costs, both direct and indirect). There are several cost-based methods of pricing.

**Markup on Full Cost** is the easiest and most frequently used pricing method, whereby the manufacturer determines **full costs** (i.e., labor, materials, and overhead) of a particular item and then adds on a percentage of those full costs as a desirable profit margin. (Note that in a **retail** business, markup is usually figured as a percentage of selling price rather than a percentage of cost.)

Selling price = Total cost per unit + Desired markup x Cost per unit

Here, markup percentage is somewhat arbitrarily determined, but attempts are made to allocate markup as a percentage of total business overhead costs.

For example,

| | | |
|---|---|---|
| Direct labor cost/unit | = | $ .10 |
| Direct materials cost/unit | = | .08 |
| Direct cost | = | $ .18 |
| Overhead/unit | = | .04 |
| Total cost | = | $ .22 |

If management agrees that a 50% markup on total costs would be desirable, then

Selling Price = $.22 + 50% ($.22) = $.33/unit
= floor price per unit $.33

**Incremental pricing** is used where the manufactured product involves high material and labor costs. The manufacturer may want to determine a floor price which emphasizes the incremental cost of producing additional units, that is, the direct cost:

Selling price = (Labor + Materials) + Markup x (Labor + Materials)

For example, suppose we use the same cost figures previously cited, then

Selling Price = ($.10 + .08) + 50% ($.10 + .08) = $.27 per unit floor price

This approach deemphasizes using overhead in determining the floor cost, assuming that overhead costs are minimal or absorbed through a comfortable profit margin on some of the manufacturer's other items.

**Conversion cost pricing** is typical in a manufacturing business where labor and overhead costs (machinery, etc.) are relatively high. The manufacturer bases prices on the value added to each incremental unit. In this case,

Selling price = (Direct labor + Overhead) + Markup x (Labor + Overhead)

Again, using the above cost figures,

Selling price = ($.10 + .04) + 50% ($.10 + .04)
= $.21 per unit floor price

As can be seen in the above examples, the floor price can vary depending upon management emphasis on various cost factors and desired profit margin.

Determining an effective ceiling price (the price above which the market is unwilling to buy) is also important in your initial pricing decision. Unless you conduct the market research or hire a market research firm, the ceiling price will be your best guesstimate. Since it's easier to lower prices than to raise them, build in a little extra profit margin at the start, as long as initial selling price will attract customers.

---

Q3-2 Determine your relevant price range:

     floor price: $ _____

     ceiling price: $ _____

---

## Pricing Strategy

If customers don't purchase according to your initial sales projections, what options are available to determine a more appropriate pricing strategy?

**Decrease price** to test for a target market ceiling. If the market is price-sensitive and the product sells, you will still need to cover costs and make a profit. Your relevant price range can be refined through trial and error in pricing strategy. To remain competitive, you will have to:

o   Lower costs (labor, material cost, or overhead) to lower the price, or

o   Accept a lower profit margin.

If the price at which customers can be attracted lies below your floor price, it will not be profitable to sell that item. At this point you may choose to stop making the item, to manufacture it as a loss leader or to round out a product line, or to differentiate the product on factors other than price.

**Product differentiation** can help you avoid competing on the basis of price. Emphasize other product features and benefits which may attract customers, even at a somewhat higher price than a competitor's item. Some of these nonprice factors include:

o   Service

o   Product availability

o   Speed of delivery

o   High quality or performance

o   Advanced technology or design

o   Satisfaction guaranteed

o   Special financing arrangements

o   Volume discounts or preferred customer status

o   Packaging differences (sizes, colors, reusable containers)

When marketing a new product, spend a minute now to figure an initial product price and check those nonprice factors which should be considered when developing a pricing strategy. Products and services that can successfully compete on nonprice factors include:

o   Those for which there are few substitutions

o   Those which are infrequently purchased

o   Those which have low impact on your customer's budget decisions

Q3-3 Describe how sales of your product or service would be affected by advertising of nonprice factors which help differentiate your product or service.

## Other Factors

There are many other factors to consider in developing a price strategy for both a service and a manufactured product.

**Company price policy** may be determined by such factors as:

o   Wanting to have a certain price reputation—the highest or lowest.

o   Catering to a particular market segment.

o   Compensating for a poor location with a company policy of 10% below the better located competition.

Q3-4 Do you have written or unwritten company policies that affect pricing policies? What are they?

**Competition** may dictate your price policy. Over the long run, certain businesses may feel that it is necessary to price according to the competition. A manufacturer or wholesaler of items similar to the competition may have little choice but to price accordingly, whereas a manufacturer of a one-of-a-kind item or one whose competitor is not in a convenient location may not have the same concerns. Professional service pricing may depend on standard fees or hourly rates, although there are many other factors in the service industry which warrant quite a price variance.

Q3-5 How significant are the prices of your competition in determining your price policy?

Business conditions are important; for example, wholesalers' prices tend to fluctuate more than manufacturers' and retailers' prices. Wholesalers deal in large quantities on a narrow margin. Manufacturers attempt to stabilize prices on their various products. Retailers have wider operating margins and it's more convenient to make changes; thus, changes are fewer but more dramatic when they do occur. Some pricing is based on basic economic conditions: if times are good, increase wealth by increasing prices; if times are bad, ignore the standard markup, cut prices and try to stay alive.

---

Q3-6 How sensitive are your prices to changes in business conditions?

---

## Market Strategy for Pricing

The best price is the one that will get the most dollars while the product or service is on the market. This may be done by going for a large volume at a low markup or high markup at low volume. Maybe you are using a loss leader technique—offering selected goods or services at or below cost to expose the customer to other items. New products are often introduced at an initial cost higher than the actual cost of production to establish the item as a quality-prestige product or service.

As this discussion illustrates, many different factors enter the process of determining price. Different combinations may be used at any point in time. Some pricing is done to reflect all direct costs (labor and materials), the allowable portion of overhead, and a percentage for profit. Cost-plus-margin pricing adds a desired percent markup to basic costs, whereas markup as a percentage of sales is the technique most frequently used in retail pricing. Some price strategy is based on the going rate. Others may utilize some form of marginal cost pricing on the assumption that some items could be sold at less than full cost but still make a positive contribution to total revenue. They may return their own variable costs and contribute some to fixed costs of the business. Market strategy may change considerably over the life of the product or service business.

Price will be a reflection of many parts of an overall marketing strategy:

o   What potential customers see as the value of the product or service.

Q3-7 What do customers believe to be the value of your product or service?




What price range (see Q2-2) will attract your target customers?

o The **direct and overhead** costs of providing the product or service, unless it is to be considered a loss leader.

Q3-8 What are the direct and overhead costs of providing the product or service?

Labor        $_____

Materials    $_____

Overhead     $_____

Total cost   $_____

o The **product** or service mixture, i.e., the batch of features which are characteristic of the product or service.

Q3-9 Does the price adequately reflect the extras you deliver or provide?


If so, how?



Q3-10 What price will you initially charge?

## Subjective Aspects

Promote your products or services to potential customers at prices which they feel good about and which also offer you a fair profit. There certainly are many subjective aspects involved in a pricing strategy. Pricing can actually influence the development of the target market as well as the quantity of product purchased or the frequency of service. Therefore, successful pricing strategy will affect the overall revenue and profit picture. While determining your pricing strategy, keep in mind the following observations about pricing characteristics. Mark each idea that you feel might be relevant to the pricing strategy.

o   Your product can be priced higher than, equal to, or less than your competition (referred to as "skimming the owner," "me too," and "market penetration" pricing, respectively).

o   It is generally easier to lower prices than to raise them. This suggests the possibility of using the skimming strategy with the introduction of a new product or service, which is acceptable because early adopters tend to have higher incomes and be relatively insensitive to price. As the product or service catches on in the marketplace, you probably will find it profitable to reduce the price in order to expand the overall target market.

o   Price conveys a certain image or perception. For instance, discount businesses often show the market or retail price with a line through it followed by a lower price which is designated as "your price," implying extra value included with the purchase.

o   Higher prices must be consistent with the environment in which the item or service is for sale and also be consistent with its perceived qualities or features. For example, charging $1.95 per pack of cigarettes may be acceptable for a 24-hour convenience store in the Nevada desert, but too much in a city supermarket. The junior partner in a law firm is usually billed at a lower rate than a senior partner.

o   Consumers in general tend to be price conscious—they value a bargain. However, they may not necessarily be price **knowledgeable**—aware of the going price for specific goods and services. This is evident in quiz shows where the contestants guess the total value of a group of items—yet they are often way off base regarding price.

o   There is a tendency among high-income consumers to be less price conscious than low-income consumers. For the high-income market, cost is neither a valued need nor a wise advertising appeal. Individuals with considerable disposable income have more time and money available to shop for specialty goods and services for which the main appeal is uniqueness rather than bargain prices.

o   The discount shopper is concerned about prices—the lower the price, the greater the perceived value and satisfaction with the purchase.

o   For many consumers, higher price implies higher quality—which isn't necessarily the case.

o   Loss leaders work well for some businesses, especially if there are other higher profit items and services available from that business.

o   Charging whatever the market will bear may be an appropriate pricing strategy for some goods and services, especially if they involve emergencies such as roadside towing service, heart transplants, tire chains, or all-night gasoline.

o   Odd pricing is psychologically preferable to even pricing for goods ($2.98 vs. $3.00), yet the reverse is often true for services ($25.00 vs. $24.98 per hour).

o   Customary pricing is good for goodwill. For example, rather than increasing the price of a go-cart ride from $1.00 to $1.25 for four minutes, an owner might charge $1.00 for a three-and-a-half-minute ride.

o   Multiple pricing (2 for $1.00 vs. 55 cents each) can be an inexpensive, yet effective marketing strategy, especially if the customer normally would buy one item. For a service such as a haircut, a 2-for-1 pricing strategy may help increase clientele, especially among family and friends.

o   The way a service is priced affects its perceived value. Intangible quantities, such as feeling good after a facial, are often perceived as being worth every penny.

o   Usually persons seeking advice or consultation are more likely to accept the advice if they have to pay for it than if it is free. However, an often-used pricing strategy to develop new clients is to offer the first consultation free or at a cut rate.

o   Pricing practice for a service is often based on an hourly rate plus expenses, both direct and indirect. The hourly rate is based upon industry or local standards, as well as upon quality of service given and degree of expertise or specialization required to perform the service. A mechanic for marine engines, for instance, may be able to charge a higher rate than an auto mechanic. Overhead expenses, such as telephone and service vehicle maintenance, must be included in the overall price structure in order to ensure a reasonable profit.

o   For products and services of a more unique nature, i.e., a commercial artist or custom home designer, it is possible to charge whatever the market will bear. Services like these are customized according to the client's desires and, therefore, are priced according to demand rather than according to a cost-plus approach.

Q3-11 How can you best describe your overall market strategy for pricing? Include subjective aspects of your pricing decision.

**Worksheet 6 Target Market Pricing Strategy**

Is my product an industrial or consumer good? (Q1-1)

Can my product can be further classified as a convenience, shopping or specialty good? (Q1-2)

My product or service has relatively (high, medium, low): (Q1-3 to 8)

    __ Relative unit cost
    __ Degree of energy spent to purchase it
    __ Degree of value to the consumer
    __ Rate of change in technology
    __ Degree/amount of training or service required
    __ Frequency of purchase

My service, as classified by service specialty, type of service provided, or type of buyer is (Q1-12)

The stage in the life cycle of my product or service is (Q1-14)

The effect on sales of a change in price of my product or service would be (Q3-1)

The effect on sales of increasing or decreasing advertising on non-price factors is (Q3-3)

The written or unwritten company policies affecting pricing policy in my company are (Q3-4)

The significance of competitors' prices on my pricing strategy is (Q3-5)

The sensitivity of my price to changes in business conditions can be described as (Q3-6)

My overall market strategy for pricing is (Q3-11)

_____

My initial pricing formula, including labor, materials, overhead, and reasonable profit, can be calculated as follows: (Q3-2, 8, 10)

| | |
|---|---|
| Labor | $_____ |
| Materials | $_____ |
| Overhead | $_____ |
| Total costs | $_____ |
| Desired profit | _____ % (of cost or retail) |
| Selling price | $_____ |

What is the value of my product or service to my customers? (Q3-7)

_____

How much price cutting do I expect? (Q3-5)

_____

My relevant price range is a floor price of $_____ to a ceiling price of $_____. (Q3-2)

_____

My suggested product or service price is $_____. (Q3-10)

_____

The subjective aspects of pricing my product or service are (Q3-11)

_____

Given my target market, my most effective market pricing strategy could be summarized as follows:

# Chapter 4
# Developing and Communicating Awareness
# of Your Product or Service

Once you have scrutinized your business, your target customer groups, and your price structure, it is time to develop a marketing plan. The next steps, to be taken in this chapter, are to set your marketing goals and to put some thought and effort into deciding what should be said in your advertising, your presenta- on, and your packaging. In short, make sure you have your message right before you examine the media, call an ad agency, or start writing commercials.

## Setting Goals

When introducing a new product or service to the marketplace, setting goals is a starting point. You will then plan to achieve those goals through developing a good marketing plan and satisfied customers. Once the target market segments have been clearly identified (refer to Worksheets 1 through 6) so that you're knowledgeable about the characteristics of the product or service and its potential customers, set specific sales and marketing goals. Your plan will aim to reach them at the end of a given period of time, such as six months or a year.

Marketing goals are designed to answer the question: What results do I expect to achieve from the marketing strategy to be developed for next year in such areas as sales, market share, growth, profit, and possible diversification?

---

Q4-1 What results are expected this year in:

  o Sales (Gross dollar amount)




  o Market share

---

o Growth


o Profitability


o Diversification potential

With the answers to these questions, you can summarize your thought and research from the previous chapters in a **sales goal statement** (Worksheet 7)

Q4-2 In what areas do you need to clarify the customer profile to achieve these goals?

Answering this question (Worksheet 8) will assure that you have all the facts you need at hand.

**Worksheet 7 Sales Goal Statement**

I want to provide _____ (Q1-1 to 8)

goods/services to _____ target customer groups (Q2-16),

whose major benefit or purpose in purchasing my product or service is _____

_____

_____(Q2-1, Worksheet 2).

I want gross sales of $_____ over the next year, with an increase in

sales of _____% per year for the next _____ years (Q4-1). This should allow

me to make $_____ per year, or at least a basic draw of $_____

per month this year (Worksheet 6).

I plan to build success on my differential advantage(s) of _____

_____

_____ (Worksheets 2 and 5).

I can then modify or expand my product or service offering, my location, my

pricing strategy, and the combination of media, sales promotion ideas, and

personal selling strategies to accomplish my long-run goals of _____

_____ (Q4-1, Worksheet 5).

_____

## Worksheet 8 Clarifying Customer Profile

| Desired Customer Profile | Actual Customer Profile |
|---|---|
| Age _____ Sex _____ | Age _____ Sex _____ |
| Area in which customer | Area in which customer |
| lives _____ | lives _____ |
| or works _____ | or works _____ |
| Income level _____ | Income level _____ |
| **Professions or occupations** | **Professions or occupations** |
| _____ | _____ |
| _____ | _____ |
| _____ | _____ |
| _____ | _____ |
| **Special interests** | **Special interests** |
| _____ | _____ |
| _____ | _____ |
| _____ | _____ |
| **Other market segment characteristics** | **Other market segment characteristics** |
| _____ | _____ |
| _____ | _____ |
| _____ | _____ |
| _____ | _____ |
| _____ | _____ |
| _____ | _____ |
| _____ | _____ |

## Developing Your Image

The purpose of developing a marketing plan for products and services is to help a business achieve a clear market position among its competitors. Not only do you want to get customers to buy NOW, but you naturally want them to buy again and again (at least certain goods and services). You also want customers to influence others to buy your goods and services through word-of-mouth and product use or service experience. Start by putting yourself in the customer's place.

> **Q4-3** Imagine your most satisfied customers telling someone else about your product or service. What would they say?

How the total sales process is seen by customers may be critical to achieving a clear market position among competitors. The many ways a product is packaged and displayed—its logo, how sales or office environment comes across to your clientele, window displays and point-of-purchase environment, location, the advertising media used, the people who represent your product or service—all affect sales now and in the long run.

> **Q4-4** Describe the sales process as seen by your customer or client.
> What things to they—or should they—perceive as they buy from you?

It is usually best to use a consistent approach in developing a market strategy. If your marketing goal is to project a high-quality image, the advertising design and media selection need to reflect high quality in order to be consistent. A health food store's grand opening advertised in a matchbook imprinted with the store name, address and phone number would be inexpensive. Would it be consistent with the image the owner wants to portray? Hardly! It would be much more effective to hand out a business card with an invitation to a free evening health lecture. This method of communicating awareness of the product or service to the target group—e.g., people who are interested in health and value it enough to purchase health goods—is much more consistent with reaching a health-conscious market.

Q4-5 What is the image you would like to project with your product
or service?

The key to good marketing positioning is to define real or perceived differences
between yours and others' products and services being offered in the same
market area, and to then interpret the differences to potential consumers as
being of benefit to them. A **perceived differential advantage** is what you want
to emphasize in planning your marketing campaign. (Review Worksheet 6)

Q4-6 How is your product or service differentiated?

All goods and services—whether intended for industrial users or final consumers—
can be differentiated in the marketplace through advertising and sales promotion
techniques. Whether the product features or service benefits being promoted are
tangible (such as the car that can come to a complete stop in two seconds from
55 mph) or intangible (such as the toothpaste which provides "sex appeal") to a
potential buyer a product or service is a complex cluster of perceived value
satisfaction.

Many businesses sell products or services which are nearly the same as their
competitors' (such as salt, cigarettes, beer, or blue jeans) in the marketplace. For
instance, Jordache brand jeans launched an expensive television advertising campaign to create a teenage target market for expensive designer jeans. These jeans
may be undifferentiated from others like them in the marketplace, except for the
media advertising promoting the brand-name label. When the actual product is
undifferentiated, the perceived product benefits (youth, sex appeal, power, status)
become the essence of the total product offering. This **total image packaging**
makes the difference in getting your target customers; product use or service
experience makes the difference in keeping them.

All of the various reasons people purchase products and services can become
useful ways to differentiate a product or service offering. It all boils down to
**packaging, presentation, and advertising.** The potential buyer attaches value to
a product or service in terms of its perceived ability to help him or her satisfy
a need or solve a problem.

Q4-7 How your product or service either satisfy a need or solve a problem?

## Product vs. Service Profile

This need or problem solution may be tangible or intangible—objective or subjective. Consider the range of possibilities from physical properties to subjective evaluations. Worksheet 9 will help you list the most important descriptive words for your product or service. Which of the following words would apply in your case? (Refer to Worksheet 2.)

For a product:
    Physical properties:
        Size—single serving—for large jobs
        Shape—to fit in the corner
        Images—fragrance, tone quality, weight
    How it performs:
        Comfort—does not pinch
        Efficiency—gets it done in less time
        Other—performance, preciseness, stability, stackability, durability
    Subjective evaluation:
        Fashionable—shows you know today's needs
        Audible—can be heard regardless of distraction
        Other—exclusive, manly, feminine

For a service:
    Purpose:
        Improvement—in speaking abilities
        Protection—from robberies
        Other—beauty, pleasure, delivery, problem solving
    Performance:
        Regularity—every week
        Durability—lasts a year
        Other—skill, experience, specialized
    Subjective evaluation:
        Efficient—in only one day
        Responsive—designed with your needs in mind
        Other—informal, courteous, attentive

**Worksheet 9 Descriptive Words for My Product or Service**

(Describe the customer needs your product or service is expected to satisfy.)

1.

2.

3.

4.

5.

6.

7.

8.

9.

10.

## Marketing Services - A Special Case

All services and most products have both tangible and intangible benefits as perceived by potential customers. Tangible benefits can usually be directly experienced—seen, smelled, tasted, touched, and tested. Intangible benefits, on the other hand, relate more directly to a projected image. There are several special characteristics of the service sector of our economy that indicate service providers may have to work a little harder to differentiate their **service package**.

Since intangible benefits are more difficult to relate to in advance, word of mouth from satisfied customers becomes a vital tool to reach other customers. Joe's tax service claims to be able to save tax dollars. You may not believe Joe, but you would believe someone who had experienced the service before and perceived that to be true.

---

Q4-8 Describe how word-of-mouth advertising is good for your business.



What could you do, if anything, to improve the quality and quantity of word-of-mouth advertising?

---

Most service purchases can easily be postponed, or often even performed by the customers themselves. Therefore, advertising appeals made to alleviate problems NOW or to bring more convenience into life will help achieve your sales target.

---

Q4-9 What appeal would help your target market alleviate one of its problems NOW?

---

Often the assessment of the value or worth of the service is made while it is being delivered or performed. The doctor moves authoritatively and speaks with conviction. The attorney moves smoothly and speaks assuringly. The analyst reels off crisp scenarios—what if this happens? The feelings developed while the service is being provided affect the assessment of its value.

> Q4-10 Describe how the delivery or performance of your service affects customers' perception of what the service is worth.
>
>
>
>
> What can be done during the process of delivery to help the customer know that the right choice has been made?

## Impacts of Different Basic Communication Tools

Every marketing strategy involves a combination of communication tools used to project an image into the marketing arena. Written promotional materials, personal contacts, and oral advertising media (like radio and television) provide opportunities to shape a product or service image and thereby affect sales.

**Visual communication tools** like the logo, location, drawings, or photographs can be made to attract customers to a product or service. The business environment of a manufacturing outlet, store, or office tells a story and creates an image (hopefully positive) in the minds of potential customers. Storefront signage, window displays, and point-of-purchase displays, all communicate a certain image, as do the clothes that a salesperson or service provider wears.

Q4-11 List some of your major visual communication tools.
What image does each communicate?

**Printed promotional materials** such as business cards, brochures, labels, and direct-mail materials all influence a total product or service package image. Advertising media such as magazines, newspapers, posters, and billboards greatly influence how a potential customer views a product or service image. Sales promotion campaigns involving contests, prizes, coupons, and free home trials can be very effective in communicating an image to the consumer.

Q4-12 Describe the printed promotional materials you use.
How does each contribute to your product or service image?

**Prices** can affect the purchase decision in ways that you might not expect. Price tags convey an image, and it may or may not be the total image needed to make the sale. Price is the customer's measure of what he or she is willing to pay in order to receive the benefits associated with the purchase. Price also affects the customers' perception of the value.

Consider the example of the couple looking for an antique clock.

When the shopkeeper was asked about the history of one clock, it matched what they had been looking for, and they expected to pay about $850. When they learned that the price was $250, Their reaction was one of disappointment; they figured at that low a price there must be something wrong with it. Their needs (for spending a certain amount to receive a sense of satisfaction) would not be met by purchasing that antique.

Other types of customers might react with different perceptions, i.e., that the purchase of such an obviously valuable item would be a real bargain. Their bargain-hunting needs would be met—a different target audience.

In the special case of services, price will likely be more related to demand than to cost. Price is thus a mechanism through which the marketeer can experiment and observe the sales increase or decrease with a change in price.

Q4-13 What image does your price convey?

Q4-14 What prices do your customers expect to pay given your location? (Refer to Worksheet 2 for these pricing questions.)

Given your quality?

Q4-15 Is price as important as selection, convenience, or quality?

Q4-16 What impact on sales would lowering or raising your price have? (Refer to Chapter 3.)

**Total Image Packaging.** One major aspect of total image packaging is the actual package itself. The logo, colors, product description, brand name, the amount to include in a given package size, the number of different sizes to package—all are part of the packaging image you have an opportunity to create. Often the first opportunity to attract a customer, the package is an essential part of creating awareness of the existence of your product or service. How many times have you been attracted to a new product or service because its name, logo, or container caught your eye? International Business Machines (IBM) used its business name in introducing a new product (the IBM Personal Computer); dress designers have become successful by developing a unique label to which people are often attracted before seeing a particular garment; children's toys are often packaged in brightly colored see-through packages to attract attention, or in no packages to let the customer see and feel them (such as stuffed animals).

Q4-17 Describe your product or service "package."

**Words Used.** The words on the package design or the business card for a service can deliver product or service description (the *all-purpose cleanser*, *express mail delivery*, *lawn care specialists*). It can also promise **intangible benefits** to attract the buyer (the perfume with *sex appeal*, for that *satisfied feeling*, the drink that makes you *feel good all over*). In fact, the words on the package, business card, office signage, or logo design can do much to position a product or service in the marketplace. The power of suggestion to buy often comes through the words:

**Location:** Last Chance Cafe—*Last Stop for Next 27 Miles*, *Eastside Tavern.*

**Audience:** The Adult Game, *For Those Who Care Enough to Send the Very Best*

**Ingredients:** *Low-Calorie Sweetener Equal to Nutra-Sweet, All Natural*

**Manufacturers:** *It's the Water—Olympia,*
*California's Finest Redwood Burl Furniture*

**Use:** *When You Don't Have Time to Cook, When You Need Variety*

**Result of Use:** *The People-Pleasing Soft Drink,*
*Faster Relief for Your Sinus Headache*

**Guarantee:** *The Only Battery Guaranteed for the Life of Your Car*

**Service:** *Factory-trained Mechanics,*
*Certified Gemologist*

---

**Q4-18 List several phrases for your product or service that will help create awareness in your target customers.**

**Worksheet 10 Visual Imaging of Your Product or Service Package**

How do you plan to create awareness of your product or service through total image packaging? Describe the specifics of the following packaging aspects:

Logo (Q4-11)

_____

Location (Q4-11, Q2-36, 37, Worksheet 4)

_____

Price strategy (Q3-4 to 10, Worksheet 6)

_____

Brand name (Q4-17, 18)

_____

Product name (Q4-18, Worksheet 9)

_____

Special features, benefits, advantages, intangibles you want to communicate to your potential customers as part of the total image package conveyed (Refer to Worksheet 2)

Sales process (Q4-4, 6, 7)

_____

Special phrase or jingle (Q4-18)

_____

Package or container design (Q4-11, 17)

_____

Colors (Q4-6, 11, 18)

_____

Sizes (Q4-17)

_____

Label design (Q4-17, 18)

_____

Business card design (Q4-5, 6, 17, 18)

_____

Business or office signage (Q4-10, 11, 18)

_____

Perceived differential advantage (Worksheet 5, Q4-3 to 7)

_____

## Developing Your Advertising Message

In developing advertising messages that support the packaging, three images are important:

o Your personal and organizational sales goals and image (see Worksheet 7)

o An up-to-date profile on the buying and lifestyle characteristics of target customer groups (see Worksheet 8)

o The tangible and intangible benefits of using your product or service (see Worksheet 2)

Your advertising message should respond to the proverbial customer question: "What's in it for me?" Your message influences the buying decision and affects your overall marketing image. People are often buying promises they've seen advertised somewhere. They buy to satisfy perceived needs, solve problems, and because they want to (impulse buying). An advertising message helps create images of benefits—desirable personal qualities (integrity, caring, budget-consciousness) and benefits of the product or service (richer texture, sex appeal, healthier)—that hopefully arouse the desire to purchase the advertised item.

**What** you choose to advertise (the specific service or product versus a cluster of related products or services) and the particular **image** your advertising creates through **pictures, words, sounds,** and **light** can have a tremendous impact on sales.

Your advertising message needs to relate to specific goals you may set such as:

o To increase store traffic or the number of service referrals (sales).

o To inform the target customers of a new product or service (demonstrations, free samples, 10-day home trial, 2-for-1 offer, sales, price rebates and discounts).

o To build your company image (quality service, "We can't be undersold and we'll prove it," "We aim to please," "The bank of active people").

o To appeal to new target groups (enticing teenagers to purchase designer jeans, attracting folks over 65 to join the health food and exercise clubs).

Your advertising message needs to **inform, persuade,** and **remind** customers that your product or service will be to their benefit—that it will satisfy their perceived need at a fair price.

The following are ways to most effectively develop your advertising message so that it reaches your target customers:

o When dealing with intangible benefits, it is especially useful to create mottoes and metaphors that the intended customer can easily remember.

o Consumers of intangible goods and services often don't know the quality of service they're receiving until something goes wrong. It is up to you to remind them what they're getting—spell out the perceived benefits by using creative pictures and words.

o The advertising message needs to be relevant to the target customers by specifying benefits that say: "My friends or family will gain something if I buy it."

o Keep the message simple and direct, since potential customers only have a few seconds to observe. Readers, listeners, and viewers often gloss over ads that don't strike them immediately.

o People are constantly bombarded with advertising from all directions in the course of a single day. The ad that is unusual will better attract attention.

o Ad layout that is simple and direct (i.e., specific benefits spelled out) and utilizes a dominant element that people can focus their attention on will attract attention easily.

o Effective headlines and sub-headlines, along with catchy phrases and tunes, symbols, or special effects can create a lasting image in the consumer's mind.

o The image projected through advertising copy is reflected in the choice of benefit-words, print size, colors (black print on white background is most effective), typography (*Olde English* projects antiquity, **heavy black** print often indicates a bargain in the offering) and other ad copy choices.

o If your brand or logo is well-recognized through previous advertising efforts, it makes sense to include this factor in the message in order to build trust, confidence, and continuity in an overall image.

o Arousing people's interest and desire is often best accomplished through the use of words and images that arouse emotions (FEAR of being robbed, not enough insurance; LOVE if you smell good or wear the right clothes; SUCCESS if you carry a leather briefcase or have a personal computer at the office).

o Clever headlines that try to trick the imagination or deceive can be misleading, so try to be creative without being difficult. Creative use of leading questions, unusual or catchy headlines, and headlines relating to local news or personalities can be useful in creating attention.

o   Avoid exaggeration and words that are overused or too generalized. Don't make specific claims that can't be demonstrated—there are laws about that.

o   Be sure to utilize "white space"—the areas of your advertising space that have no pictures or words (or sound). People remember ad copy better and more vividly if the total ad space is not filled with words.

o   Avoid distracting techniques, but try to use demonstrations whenever possible to get audience or reader participation and involvement.

o   Testimonials are great "word-of-mouth" advertisements and can be effective especially when the commercial is presented by a well-known personality who lends a certain character to the advertising image.

o   Provide immediate benefits to potential customers—offer them specials like "free home trial," "guaranteed for life," and "the best that money can buy."

o   Use words and images to create a concept of "value" that will justify the price.

o   Don't forget essentials such as the company name, phone number, address, and brand name or logo.

o   Ask for the sale—close the sale with customers after familiarizing them with your product or service benefits by asking them to "send check or money order," "act NOW," "write now for free information and coupons."

Although you may want to design the advertising message, appoint an employee or associate to handle that task, or even hire an outside advertising agency to help bring the message to the target groups with a degree of professionalism. (The topic is part of Chapter 6.) If you are interested in developing your talents along this line, there are a host of books, seminars, and tapes available that teach how. Help is usually available through media representatives and their organizations. Help is also frequently available through a local college or university, or a marketing or advertising consultant who can freelance marketing talents.

**Worksheet 11 Planning an Effective Advertising Message
to Support the Total Image Packaging**

Write the key words, headlines, sub-headlines, major product or service benefits you want the target customers to know about you, the product or service, or the organization in general.

How do you plan to organize your message so that it attracts:

Attention

Interest

Desire

Action

Is your ad layout:

Creative? Describe how

Unique? Describe in which ways

Specified (product/service/groupings)

Believable? In what ways

Understandable? Describe image created

Distinctive typeface? Which type

Brand identified?

Logo/company name identified?

Written with customer in mind? How?

Size

Location (on page, time slot) best suited to get attention?

Illustration?    Graphic design utilized?

White space utilization?

Basic information included?
   Product brand name or logo

   Address

   Telephone/800 number

   Special offer deadlines

   Product or service guarantees

Emotional appeal?

Human interest appeal?

Other ad layout factors?

# Chapter 5
# Media Alternatives

Most entrepreneurs use a variety of advertising and sales promotion techniques to help achieve essential market awareness. Advertising and sales promotion go hand in hand as part of an overall marketing strategy. Through **advertising media** such as radio, television, newspapers, magazines, and trade journals you can attract customers to you. **Sales promotions,** coupons, direct mail flyers, publicity, public relations, personal selling, and point-of-purchase displays can be effective communications tools to turn interested potential buyers into actual customers.

> **Q5-1 List the advertising and sales promotion techniques you have used or are thinking about using. (See Q4-8, 11, 12)**

All advertising and sales promotion efforts are directed toward the following purposes:

o   To sell.

o   To identify the company, its product, or services.

o   To present product features or service benefits that will appeal to the target customers.

o   To identify the place and price of the goods and services.

o   To offer specials, such as product samples, two-for-one sales, or reduced prices, in an effort to attract customers or deplete inventories.

o   To attract new customers or generate prior customer support for your product or service.

o   To keep a trade name fresh in the minds of customers until they need your product or service again.

o   To promote your differential advantage, distinguishing your company and its products or services from competitors.

o   To build confidence, promote goodwill, and speed up inventory turnover.

o   To reinforce customers' needs for your product or service.

> Q5-2 Which three of the above ideas are the most important ones for you?

## Advertising Media Value Comparison

When measuring the **value** of various media, the standard method of comparison is to establish **cost per thousand people** exposed to the advertising message. This figure is computed the same way for any medium:

Cost per thousand (CPM)

$$= \frac{\text{Amount of money spent}}{\text{People Exposed to Your Message}} \times 1000$$

Example:

$$= \frac{\$12,000 \text{ ad cost}}{2,000,000 \text{ people exposed}} \times 1000$$

$$= \quad \$.006 \text{ per person} \quad \times 1000$$

$$= \quad \$6 \text{ cost}/1000 \text{ (CPM)}$$

The value must take into consideration whether the medium reaches the target customers, or just lots of people.

## Television

Television audiences tend to change channels frequently as their favorite programs come on, so advertising space is targeted to audiences that watch specific programs. Audience surveys are readily available with specific information about the composition of the audience of a particular station at any given time. The two best known are the *Nielsen Station Index* and the *Arbitron Index.*

The greatest selectivity of audiences for television revolves around combinations of specific times of day or night and specific programs that reach a particular viewer segment. **Housespouse** time runs from early morning sign-on until 4:00 p.m. the **early evening fringe** runs from 4:00 until 6:30 p.m., **prime time** is from 6:30 until 10:30 p.m., and the **late night fringe** runs from 10:30 until **sign-off.** Prime time is most expensive, since it has the greatest total number of viewers on any channel. But your particular target audience may be primarily housespouses, and your advertising dollars may be more effectively spent in the housespouse time period.

Often, just the fact that you're using television—the glamour and prestige medium—can add perceived or intangible value to the product or service. People use their **eyes and ears** in receiving a television commercial so that it becomes a very powerful communication tool. Program your audience to see what you want, when you choose, with a message that grabs their attention. If the product or service has mass appeal, television is an excellent advertising medium to demonstrate both real and perceived benefits. If the product takes a long time to demonstrate effectively, however, a 30-second or 60-second ad may not be enough time, and this expensive medium may then be relatively ineffective.

**Advantages**

o Glamorous, exciting, full of impact.

o Utilizes a multisensory way of promoting your message.

o Visual techniques create uniqueness and reinforce memory.

o Enhances the company or corporate image as part of the packaging.

o Creates credibility in viewers' minds through utilization of famous people hired to help promote a product or service.

Q5-3 What would be the advantages of using television to advertise your product or service? Which channels?

**Disadvantages**

o Expensive (commercial production costs often vary from several hundred to several thousand dollars). A 30-second spot on national television could cost over $100,000.

o Can become complex, i.e., using different emphases within the same 60-second commercial, using special effects and animation.

o Doesn't allow viewer to refer back to the message when he or she is facing a buying decision.

o Viewer receptivity can be limited, even during costly prime time, since people often leave during commercial breaks.

o The viewer may develop a bad attitude about all commercials as an interruption.

Q5-4 What are some potential disadvantages of you using television to advertise?

## Radio

Radio advertisements are most effective for short, repeat commercials. They are potentially less expensive than television time as measured in cost-per-thousand. Most households usually have more than one radio. The listener tends to select one station that has a favorite type of music, a talk show, or call-in program. Unlike television watchers, radio listeners tend to keep doing whatever they're doing during commercials, thus allowing the advertisement to be heard many times throughout the day or week.

A major advantage of radio is that the listening audience can be targeted much more specifically than television. This is because local radio stations program themselves to appeal to particular groups measured by the Nielsen and Arbitron Indexes. The interests or buying habits of listeners to those stations can be predicted to some degree so that your advertising dollar is well targeted.

Radio also offers great flexibility. An advertising message can be **pre-taped** (to allow sound effects and assure professionalism) or can be read live from a fact sheet from which the announcer or disk jockey ad libs. The use of a fact sheet has the advantage of communicating with the target audience in a personable manner through a personality who has become known to the listener. An image of intimacy or personal interest in your product or service can be created that is often not possible with television.

Since the lead time needed to broadcast a radio advertisement is usually not more than 72 hours, take advantage of radio to advertise with little advance notice. This can be particularly important if your competitor starts an advertising campaign that you want to counter. The expense involved in producing an advertisement may be minimal (the disk jockey's creative time versus the cost of producing a professional advertisement). This low cost adds to the desirability of radio as an effective advertising medium. Cost itself is also flexible: you can usually purchase time in 10, 20, 30, 45 and 60-second spots. Rates are also based on how many customers the station reaches. For example, the most expensive radio spot ads are during the morning and evening rush hours because automobile drivers are a captive audience.

Most radio media strategies involve utilizing spot ads on several stations within a local programming area to reach several target market segments. If you are developing an image to appeal to teens, working adults, and retired persons (a special writing pen, a photo service, a bookstore), careful selection of radio stations and a good fact sheet to the announcer can greatly help achieve market awareness. The more spots purchased, the less each will cost. Therefore, it might be beneficial to purchase time on several stations for three months to one year. By submitting a fact sheet to several station announcers, your advertising message will be interpreted to suit that station's audience. This provides direct and personal appeal to your chosen market segments.

## Advantages

o   Radio is a personal medium that reaches its audience directly through familiar station announcers and disk jockeys.

o   The listener to a particular radio station will absorb some part of an advertising message because there is a tendency to continue activities without turning off or tuning out the advertising message.

o   Radio allows more selectivity in choosing a target audience than does television, although less selectivity than direct mail.

o   There is more flexibility in the use of time and money to get an advertising message on the air.

o   It is easier to take advantages of special opportunities without having to plan ahead as much as for other media.

o   Developing special advertising jingles and repetitive messages helps potential customers recognize your product and reinforce your message.

o   Radio is a medium of immediacy, i.e., the buying response is often immediate, making your ad effectiveness measurable.

---

Q5-5 What major advantages could radio advertising offer? Which station would be most effective in reaching potential customers?

---

**Disadvantages**

o   Specific geographical targeting may be difficult, especially if the broadcast carries for many miles.

o   There is no visual impact as there is with television, magazines, or newspapers to help reinforce your advertising message.

o   Money can be wasted when trying to reach specific target customers due to audience overlap.

o   You may need to rely on the creativity of announcers to deliver your message and develop your image.

---

Q5-6  What major disadvantages would radio have for advertising your product or service?

---

## Writing a Radio Commercial

If you decide to use radio advertising, the radio station staff will often help develop the message; however, advance planning by utilizing the following question format will help clarify important message points. (A worksheet follows for creating radio advertising for your business.)

In a very short period of time your copy can address:

WHO?   Pitch to the major **target market** (*Attention Smokers*). Mention the company's name as often as possible. Repetition is good to reinforce memory and if someone tunes in late (physically or mentally). Some part of the ad may catch the listener's ear well into the commercial.

WHAT?   About the product or service—its niche? What benefits does it provide—what will the product or service do for them? (*Remove stain without scrubbing*)

WHERE?   Identify the location of the business; help the listeners find the product or service. Use action words. (*Get to Mike's at the corner of 5th and Main—take Main one block north of the Municipal Stadium.*)

WHEN?   Is this available? How long? Beginning when?

WHY?   Why buy this now? Any additional enticement? (*Scott Hamilton will autograph free pictures of his winning ice skating for today only.*)

HOW?   How can the listener get it, buy it, find it, easily? (*Call this number right now.*)

Using the guidelines above, write a radio commercial on the following worksheet. Then read it aloud. Is it easily understood? How long does it take to read?

**Worksheet 12 Radio Copy Format**

Company name

Contact

Product/Service description

Address                          Telephone number

Target audience

Copy content—major points to be covered (Who? What? Where? When? Why? How?)

Note: Any special instructions to radio announcer?

## Newspapers

More money is spent in newspaper advertising each year than in any other medium. In general, newspapers contain local advertising. In fact, for urban newspapers and weekly shoppers, advertising is almost entirely local. Such advertising offers greater selectivity in reaching a target market than either television or radio. Most newspapers have circulations that are daily, weekly, or Sunday; all offer a great opportunity to expand sales through advertising.

Valuable customer targeting can be gained through ad placement in special reader sections such as sports, business, features, or women's pages. For example, if you are selling executive calendars the best place may be the business section; the introduction of a new haircutting service for children may get better results in the women's section.

Newspaper readers' habits can be used to advantage. Readers tend to turn first to the section that interests them most. This presents an opportunity for your ad to catch their eye in relation to the editorial content they enjoy. Newspapers have the distinct advantage of being able to provide greater detail over longer periods of time than any other advertising medium, with the possible exception of magazines. Today most people rely on their local newspaper for local and regional news. People enjoy reading about their locality and the people they know. Many readers look forward to the weekend shopping specials and rely on the newspaper to introduce new retail products and service outlets. Because of their local nature, newspapers are very effective in creating awareness of a location. They are often used to make comparison shopping between different products and services. Automobile dealerships, major retail outlets, real estate agencies, and supermarkets rely heavily on the newpaper.

Classified ads work well to fill a need that already exists in the reader's mind. Therefore, classified advertising is suited to target a readership that is ready, willing and able to purchase—Now! Out of every ten classified shoppers who buy, two are impulse buyers and eight have definitely planned to buy the kind of item they purchased.

Space devoted to display advertising is usually a larger part of the advertising space in the paper. As a rule of thumb, the larger the display ad, the greater the sales impact. It may be more effective to place one large display ad in the Sunday paper rather than to buy a small space every other day during the week. Trial and error and observing the space buying habits of your competitors will help you develop an idea of what will work best for your company.

Newspaper advertising space is usually purchased by the dimensions of depth (number of lines) and width (number of columns). As an industry standard, there are 14 agate lines to the column inch, no matter how wide the column is.

For example, assume you want to buy display space that is two columns wide and six inches deep. This amounts to a space that is 2 x 6 = 12 column inches. To determine the number of agate lines, multiply the number of column inches by 14. If the cost of the advertisement is $1.00 per agate line, display advertising in the preceding example would cost $168.00 (12 column inches x 14 agate lines/inch x $1.00 per agate line).

Other factors influencing the cost of display advertising are affected by the publisher's pricing policies. Policies vary but are usually affected by competition from other newspapers regarding total amount of space purchased during a year, based on a contract or multiple insertion basis. In addition, prices change due to the amount and nature of the newspaper's readership. Neighborhood shoppers gazettes offer cheaper rates than do big city newspapers because their readership is more limited, yet this may be exactly what is needed to attract local customers to a new local business. It is important to calculate the cost of advertising per 1000 readers reached by the newspaper.

**Advantages**

o  Almost every geographic location in the United States has at least one local newspaper that can quickly respond to your advertising needs.

o  Materials given for ad insertion usually take less lead time than in other media.

o  Readers look forward to browsing through their newspaper and have become habituated to using display and classified advertising to help do their comparative shopping.

o  The quick response to a sales message can help deplete unwanted inventories or introduce new products and services.

o  The selectivity of neighborhood papers offers a low-cost opportunity to try different ad copy aimed at different audiences to test various advertising approaches.

o  Newspapers offer a less intrusive advertising forum than either television or radio, and people can refer back to specific ads.

o  There is great flexibility in ad placement and timing that allows the entrepreneur time to respond to his or her competition and changing market conditions.

o  Newspapers allow the greatest opportunity to reduce expenses through cooperative advertising allowances from manufacturers.

Q5-7 How would newspaper advertising be especially advantageous to you?

What are the most appropriate newspapers?

## Disadvantages

o   Newspapers suffer from the same clutter problems as do other media. Unless an ad is creative and stands out from others, it may not reach a particular target market.

o   If the reader is in a hurry, the editorial content may attract most attention at the expense of the advertising space.

o   Most newspapers ads are black and white, eliminating the ability to attract interest if the product is colorful.

o   Newsprint is porous and doesn't permit some ads to reproduce well.

Q5-8 What are some of the disadvantages that newspaper advertising might have for you? How could they be overcome?

## Magazines

One of the greatest benefits of magazine advertising is that full-color displays and special effects can be utilized. Like other print media, magazines rely on a visual impact rather than an aural one like radio. Therefore, the sales approach must be conceptualized differently. Since magazines are now produced to appeal to geographic regions or a specific interest group, small businesses can effectively promote a product or service probably at a lower cost than by using television or daily newspapers.

Advertising in a national magazine has the same prestige as national television advertising. People assume that advertisers in national publications have reliable and high-quality products and services. It is possible to have the prestige of a national publication but keep the cost and exposure to a regional basis by using regional editions, available from many national magazines.

The opportunities of magazines are increasing through specialization as well as regional issues. Special interest groups (teens, business owners, homeowners, women) and special fields of interest (showbusiness, computers, gardening) are now the norm. For example, over 50 publications cater to users of small computers. This trend offers marketeers greater precision in reaching the special interest groups that would most likely buy their offerings.

If you want to reach people who manage rubbish disposal and supply equipment for that industry, *Solid Waste* magazine might be appropriate. If you want to reach auto builders, dealers or associated prospects, possibly *Automotive Age* is the answer. If your message is geared to supermarket personnel, *Progressive Grocer* could be your key. Do you want to address the quick stop mini market outlets? Try *Convenience Store News.* Want to hit the people who put things in spray cans? *Aerosal Age* could do it.

**Advantages**

o   Magazines are likely to be passed along to many other readers who don't necessarily buy the magazine since they are normally kept around the house or office, sometimes for a year or more.

o   Magazines are often reread many times by potential customers who may take time to reach a buying decision and can be positively reinforced to buy each time they see the advertisement.

o   Advertising costs and media contacts can be easily researched at the public library in the *Standard Rate and Data Service (SRDS)* magazine directory.

o   Magazines can provide vivid color displays and special creative effects that support a visual image in the reader's mind.

---

Q5-9  What specific advantages could magazine advertising provide?

---

Q5-10  Which local and national magazines might be appropriate for advertising your product or service?

**Disadvantages**

o   The planning required for insertion of display advertisements requires two or more months lead time.

o   Since many magazines are published monthly or quarterly, the opportunity for rapid response or followup on successful advertising is limited.

o   Since many people read more than one magazine in their field of interest, advertising in several magazines may duplicate circulation coverage, thereby reducing dollar effectiveness and increasing cost per thousand exposed.

o   Magazines are more effective in promoting overall marketing image than for special purposes such as sales.

---

Q5-11  What disadvantages, if any, do you see in the magazines listed as appropriate?


How could these disadvantages be overcome?

---

## Yellow Pages and Business and Services Directories

Every American community has its phone book, and many communities often have other business directories. For many small businesses, the major form of advertising is the telephone book. Beauty salons, barbershops, plumbers, air conditioning, and appliance repair firms, for example, rely heavily on the *Yellow Pages* for customers. Since the *Yellow Pages* are published only once a year, listing your business under more than one category, although more expensive, is often an effective advertising strategy.

**Advantages**

o   *Yellow Page* advertising is the primary form of advertising for many small businesses because it may be very effective in cost per thousand readers reached.

o   Every home and business has a telephone book. Most people are conditioned to use the *Yellow Page* listings for locating the product or service they need.

**Disadvantages**

o   Planning is necessary to include display advertising before the deadline. Opening a new business cannot necessarily be timed to the publishing of the *Yellow Pages.*

o   Telephones for the business must be connected and paid for many months prior to publication of the *Yellow Pages.*

o   Consumers may not know the product is available or what listing it would be under. How would you look up worms for your garden, for instance?

o   It may be too much to spend for a small business, especially one whose target market is within a very short distance.

---

Q5-12  How would advertising in the *Yellow Pages* or local business
       directory be beneficial to your business?


What categories would you list under?

---

## Signs and Displays

Everyone is accustomed to reading signs wherever they go—indoors and outside. Signs of all sorts help identify your image in a potential customer's mind. They are on the job round-the-clock for anyone who passes by to observe. They create impressions, awareness, reminders that your business is available to fill customer needs. People tend to rely on signs and displays to help locate a business or display a product within a business.

---

Q5-13  Is your office or store easy to find?
       Is any additional signage needed to help find your business or help
       advertise it?

---

Q5-14 Is a billboard advertisement an effective means of advertising for you?

Why or why not?

Unlike billboards, outside storefront or office signage is sited only at the place of business. You want people to find the business, even if it's on the 15th floor. For manufacturing, wholesale, or retail outlets, a storefront sign is often the first image the passerby sees. The impression should be positive, identifiable, and associated with whatever is offered. A fleeting moment can certainly be used creatively to attract passers-by through the use of neon, special lighting, or lettering effects.

Other forms of outdoor advertising include transit posters on buses (both inside and outside the bus), taxis, commuter trains and subways, and transit station walls. Poster displays can be very creative and colorful and can reproduce well, indicating an image of quality. They are relatively inexpensive considering the daily commuters who become a captive audience for the advertising message.

**Advantages**

o   Signs, poster displays, and billboards can be extremely effective advertising media for promoting awareness of various products and services which appeal to a large mass market, as cost per thousand viewers is very reasonable.

o   Physically they are the largest form of advertising available and therefore can truly impress the passer-by.

o   Storefront and office signage are essential to helping interested customers locate and remember you.

o   They support and reinforce other forms of advertising that are part of your current marketing strategy.

o   Color reproduction is possible, and the use of illumination and spectacular special effects (especially on large, well-located billboards) can create a unique and lasting image.

**Disadvantages**

o   Billboards should be located in high traffic count areas to be effective. There may be a wait in high demand areas.

o   Billboards and signage must be unobstructed and tilted correctly on the traffic side of the road to be effective.

o   Transit advertising is easily vandalized.

o   Billboards must be attention-getting, succinct, and bold.

o   Often highly regulated—in some areas storefront signage is limited in size and visibility by local ordinance.

Q5-15 What are the legal restrictions on the types of signs you can have outside your business?



Describe the signage of your major competitor



Describe an ideal sign for your place of business

## Indoor Signs and Displays

Indoor signs have the same basic purpose as outdoor ones—to provide information about your product and service offerings and their location. Point-of-purchase displays (unless they involve special expensive production techniques) are an extremely cost-effective means of not only creating awareness of your product or service but also of enticing customers to purchase—NOW! There is no need to schedule advertising in advance.

In a local neighborhood store, window signs and displays can create awareness in passers-by and are very effectively used by the small business owner as a means of promoting new products or services, sales or end-of-season closeouts. Window displays can also be used to create a store atmosphere which is inviting (for example, holiday window displays at Halloween, Thanksgiving, and Christmas). Window displays offer a way of promoting visually many products at a time, thereby increasing effective use of selling space. Displays can be changed frequently. Customers often ask for a product "just like the one in the window."

Point-of-purchase displays can be effectively tied to your current advertising in your local newspaper or radio station. ("Look for the happy clown display at our store") The display both directs customers, drawn by the ad, to the product and reinforces their intention to buy.

The best use of point-of-purchase display involves placing it in a high traffic area at a height (often on the counter, in the entrance way, or at the cash register) where customers can clearly identify it. This form of advertising should definitely emphasize purchasing—NOW! Many magazines that are advertised on television, for instance, suggest looking for them at the grocery store checkout stand where there is a corresponding magazine rack. For a service organization, such as a dry cleaning establishment, a point-of-purchase display might describe other services (such as tailoring) available by appointment for a fee.

**Advantages**

o In-house signs and point-of-purchase displays are an inexpensive way of supporting correlated media advertisements.

o Signs can also be utilized to prompt sales of items not advertised concurrently in other media.

o The use of signs is available to every shopkeeper and service outlet.

o Window displays and point-of-purchase displays are extremely flexible since they can be changed often.

o Signs can serve as a kind of roadmap within the location to inform and attract customers and invite them to try a sample of the product as a purchase incentive.

**Disadvantages**

o Displays need to be interesting, exciting, creative, and informative without cluttering the window or counter.

o The manufacturer or wholesaler cannot be assured that the point-of-purchase display will be kept in good shape or located in a high traffic area. Many good displays end up under the counter, in the trash can, or behind some obstacle, unused.

o The displays are not always timely—the sign needs changing the day after special event. For example, after Valentine's Day the candy display keeps advertising even if all items are gone.

Q5-16 Describe how indoor signs or displays can be used to advantage for your business.

## Direct Mail

Mail-order catalogs are a form of advertising medium all their own for many manufacturers, wholesalers, and retailers. Service businesses can utilize flyers to announce their existence at a low cost to a very specific target audience (for instance, the new tax service in the shopping center). Informational brochures about local community services (such as house-sitting, gardening, remodeling) are often mailed to neighborhood mailboxes and may be filed away with a feeling of local contact and familiarity when it comes time to purchase the needed service.

The message presented on a flyer or brochure may describe your business, explain an expensive complicated new product, give detailed benefits of your service, provide technical specifications—whatever is too much for a mass-media ad.

Certain things not usually advertised in other media, such as household hints, consumer awareness blurbs, recipes, sports tips, and coupons for free trial offers can also be offered through flyers and announcements. They are more likely to remain in the prospective buyers' possession until they need what is offered. Flyers can be inexpensively handed out instead of mailed.

One of the major reasons business people like direct-mail advertising is that they can target their message to specific groups by purchasing mailing lists. As long as the lists are kept up to date you will probably reach the target markets. (Actually, these mailing lists are usually for rent and are updated by the mail list service.) For most businesses, the best mailing list is of their current customers. Use receipts, customer logs, and sign-up sheets to keep track of customers over the years.

Although direct-mail is the most expensive in terms of cost per thousand, it may often be the most effective means of advertising because of the unusually high response rate this medium can create. By controlling the time of mailing, the mailing list, the product offerings, pricing, and benefits, you can discover what works best to promote a particular product or service.

Direct-mail catalogs are their own form of business—essentially a business organization in a book that is distributed door-to-door or via the mail. Since catalogs are used as reference books, they tend to be kept on the shelf (both at home and business). They are valuable in retail outlets (remember how Sears Roebuck, Montgomery Ward, Neiman-Marcus, and J.C. Penney supported their retail sales from the start), wholesale businesses (which may develop their own product catalogs), and manufacturers who produce a line of products and utilize a catalog to create awareness of their product prices, specifications, warranties, etc.

Organizations that rely heavily on catalogs and direct-mail for their business often spend 50% or more of their total annual sales on direct-mail campaigns. The expense can be enormous—but so can the profits, as attested to by all the books and pamphlets on "How to Make a Million in Mail Order." For many businesses, mail-order IS their business—an entire way of life (often started out of a home initially). In fact, estimates are that up to 20% of all advertising dollars are spent on direct-mail advertising—over $11 billion annually. (The annual Publishers Clearing House, *Reader's Digest,* and other major direct-mail campaigns attempt to reach every household in the country with prizes and contests as incentives to purchase their product offerings).

## Advantages

o   Direct mail advertising offers the benefit of being more measurable than any other major medium.

o   It offers a high degree of flexibility (any size, color, shape, amount of small print).

o   You can utilize direct-mail to test the same basic ad with different ad copy or design to see what pulls the best response.

o   People often associate mail-order catalogs and direct-mail flyers and coupon envelopes with bargain values due to low company overhead.

o   Many people respond to the excitement of a percentage discount (10% quantity discount or 50% discount if you purchase by a certain date, for example) or the opportunity for a free trial.

o   This is a highly selective medium because you can decide who will receive your mailer through the rental of highly selective mailing lists or selective distribution of handbills to desirable target customers.

o   Advertising can be mailed at any time, without the hassle of planning ahead for copy deadlines, as is needed with other media.

**Disadvantages**

o   From the moment the mail arrives or the flyer is distributed, it may have the undivided attention of a potential customer. However, direct-mail advertisements need to be catchy and informative enough to maintain the customer's attention long enough to respond—or they can easily end up in the wastepaper basket.

o   Unless the mailing list is both up to date and reliable in terms of its categorization (age, sex, profession, lifestyle characteristics, etc.), money is wasted. Up to 25% of most lists require an address change within a given year.

o   Someone has to stuff envelopes (a hassle overcome by hiring out the distribution service or postering service).

If even 2% of the people who get your mailer order from you purchase your product or servuce, that is quite good.

---

Q5-17 Describe a direct-mail campaign that would be effective for your firm.

How would you get a mailing list? What is the cost?

---

## Special Promotions and Specialty Advertising

Special promotional advertising can take many different forms. Examples of special promotion items are calendars, pens, pencils, balloons, key chains, T-shirts, visors or hats, and measuring devices. Almost anything that you can imprint and pass out to potential customers will help support other advertising efforts. These items are considered "freebies" to the customer and are often enjoyed just for that reason—everyone feels good about receiving something useful for free.

This promotional medium is flexible and often very inexpensive due to the low-cost nature of items given away and the opportunity the business person has to obtain quantity discounts. Include the company name, phone number and address, and perhaps a catchy motto or phrase that target customers will remember in developing a unique image of the business. For example, one midwestern manufacturer of precision tube-bending equipment gave out a good quality ballpoint pen inscribed with the company name, logo, and motto: "We bend to please." It was frequently referred to by customers as a useful item that they enjoyed receiving with each sales order. Pens tend to get left on tables and passed along—and thereby contribute to your overall marketing strategy.

Other special promotions include special incentives to entice manufacturers and retailers to promote the product. These might include special coupons, trading stamps, two-for-one offers, a manufacturer's rebate, contests among sales personnel, cash bonuses and awards, free vacations, special offers on related products and services, volume and frequency of purchase discounts—and many other possibilities.

Offering various kinds of special sales incentives to people who help promote your particular product or service is not only a morale booster, but can truly help increase sales. A trip for two to Jamaica is a sales promotion package to offer the top salesperson of the month, for instance. Special discounts to youth groups and senior citizens offer incentives for these groups to buy your product (a movie, for example) or your service (a haircut and shampoo) that they might not necessarily buy otherwise.

Special in-store promotions should, of course, be supported through other media such as storefront banners, point-of-purchase displays and demonstrations, promotional literature or handouts, floor displays, or shopping bags (especially for holidays). These kinds of special promotions should have a beginning and an end so that they create excitement with other people in your distribution channels, sales personnel, and potential customers.

**Advantages**

o    There is a great deal of variety possible for special sales promotions at the product distribution level, retail level, and consumer level.

o    Whatever is offered as a sales incentive to the distributor, the retailer, or the customer involves a relatively small expense for the extra dollars brought into your organization.

o    They can help shape your total image in the marketplace through creating excitement, incentive, and a distinction in the eyes of your distributors, sales personnel, and potential customers.

**Disadvantages**

o    Special sales promotions should relate your product or service offerings to the total image you want to create.

o    Special promotions need to be well-timed in relation to other advertising efforts.

Q5-18 List some specialty promotion ideas that would help sell your product or service.

## Public Relations and Publicity

Good public and community relations involves projecting that certain image you want to achieve in the marketplace. Public relations (PR) is usually a free or inexpensive way for the small business person to get his or her name, product or service, or business happening into public awareness. By creating recognition of various new or positive aspects of your business—for instance, joining organizations like Rotary, Toastmasters, business and professional associations, creating a memorable grand opening for a new retail outlet, announcing tours through the manufacturing plant—you are helping to support whatever advertising dollars are spent on an image.

The ways in which good public relations are created varies with your location and the local media available. Join fraternal organizations, community involvement groups, and networking business lunch or dinner groups. Invite the media personalities to hear you speak at the local community college, attend a lecture, see a slide presentation at the community center—anything you're involved in that can help give your business mileage through positive publicity and community involvement.

Q5-19 List the organizations and associations to which you currently belong.

What additional organizations or memberships should you consider joining? (These might be business, recreational, religious, educational, professional or other organizations.)

Public relations and good publicity can often be developed around a unique community event, new office, employee, or promotion. The story (or press release) can be built around just about any product or service aspect, as long as it's timely or newsworthy, as the following examples suggest:

"Veterinarian makes house calls;" "odd-jobs person has over 200 tools in truck capable of handling any job—continues to buy one tool a week;" "stationery shop sells school tablets with child's picture on cover;" "she started her business selling classmates clothes she had mixed and matched from throwaways and second-hand store items;" "the partners design expandable/collapsible chairs for public places—with practically a flick of the finger the height of the chair noiselessly increases or decreases by as much as a foot."

### Advantages

o   Publicity in the news media is **free** to those who can create enough interest or newsworthiness to obtain an interview or writeup.

o   A good source of creativity if the source is consistent with your image.

o   The newsworthy nature of the product or service can be developed into a column for a newspaper or magazine.

o   Public relations and publicity can be effectively utilized to shape a total image.

---

**Q5-20 Use your brainstorming ability and ask your customers, friends, and suppliers to help identify a newsworthy item.**

---

### Disadvantages

o   Publicity generated by a special event (an open house, a speech) can be interpreted in the media according to the writer's viewpoint-which isn't always what you had in mind.

o   The newsworthy story or event must be true in order to build customer trust, loyalty, and integrity.

o   Hiring a public relations firm or agent can vary greatly in cost. The effects of good public relations and publicity are difficult to measure.

---

**Q5-21** Write a brief publicity statement about yourself, your organization, or some unique aspects of the products or services you offer for sale.

---

## Writing a Press Release

Media attention for a newsworthy item is often gained through a press release, written by someone in your organization or an agency and sent directly to various media representatives (local radio and television stations and newspapers).

When writing a press release, remember the following points:

o   **Whom to contact for more information**—first item at the top of the page. Include name, address and telephone number.

o   **Release date**—usually "For Immediate Release."

o   **Headline**—short descriptive summary of what is in the press release in four to twelve factual words.

o   **Body of press release**—details of who, what, where, why, when given in first paragraph. Keep it short and simple. A few additional paragraphs may add less important details. Include information on what readers can do if interested, such as buying tickets, ordering tapes, reserving space, securing catalogs.

o   **Typed, double-spaced**—one to two pages at most. Send an original or good photocopy, not a carbon.

o   **Determine where to send it.** If this is an item of interest to people who fish, maybe a fishing magazine would be appropriate, or maybe your local paper or radio or television station. Is this something that the publication or program usually covers? Are you after professional or trade reputation or an increase in customers? Who are your customers? What media do they watch, read or listen to?

o   **Identify the name of a specific person** to receive your news release. Magazines and periodicals list specific editors of different sections (e.g. "Lifestyles," "Business," "Sports," "Around the Town," "Education."). Call the radio and television stations to determine the name of a current publicity or public relations person. Your local business library may have directories such as *Ayres* and *Standard Rate and Data (SRDS)* which can locate a contact person.

o   **Follow up.** After a week, call. Determine if the material was received and can be used. If it isn't being used, determine why not.

o   **Be prepared for an interview,** either with someone from your organization or with satisfied customers who might be willing to have their names used as examples of past successes.

## Sample Press Release

Contact: Mike Harrigan          **FOR IMMEDIATE RELEASE**
        Out of State College Advisors
        6832 Rozak Street
        Dallas, Texas 75081
        (214) 697-0048

### COUNSELING FOR COLLEGE BOUND GETS VISUAL AID

DALLAS - Mike Harrigan is Texas' first freelance college counseler with an additional first. A former admissions officer at Harvard, Harrigan and two colleagues run Out of State College Advisors, a private service which provides, in addition to current information, video shorts showing campus life on over 100 campuses in the United States.

"My purpose is to give the eager college-bound student visual information as well as the current written information about other colleges and universities. The student can sit in on classes, visit dorms, see professors, all in one central facility," says Harrigan. "High school counselors try to inform students of opportunities. I just have the visual resources and the time to work one-on-one to match up the students' abilities, needs and wants with what is available."

The counseling session includes discussion of test scores, grade points, extracurricular activities and career planning issues. Decisions can then be made about what is the best combination of an affordable and desirable college. The fee structures are based on the extent of counseling desired. For more information call Mike Harrigan at (214) 697-0048.

- 30 -

**Worksheet 13 Press Release Format**
   (Refer to Worksheets 11 and 12 and Q5-19, 20, 21)

FOR IMMEDIATE RELEASE

CONTACT

ORGANIZATION

ADDRESS

PHONE NUMBER

HEADING

BODY

ACTION READER CAN TAKE

List newspapers, radio, TV, magazines, periodicals to send it to.

Identify one major source and major contact person.

When do you plan to mail this?

Follow-up call?

Preparation for follow-up interview?

## Trade Shows, Fairs, Demonstrations, Professional Meetings

Trade shows, fairs, or large gatherings of similar types of businesses or services offer real potential for seeing the latest fashions or newest ideas (in computer hardware or software for instance), and being seen by those most interested in finding out about you and your product or service. Buyers and sellers have an opportunity in a concentrated time and space to see what is available.

Professional organizers lease or rent a facility and usually plan the promotion. They rent out booths or display spaces. A software game designer had no idea how to market his product. He was able to demonstrate the game at a computer trade show. One of the major producers of computers expressed an interest. It was a firm that had told him over the telephone on initial inquiries that they were not interested.

Book publishers such as Oasis Press rent a booth at professional meetings or at trade shows where people who talk about small business or who have their own small business are meeting. Sign-up sheets secure names on permanent mailing lists. Complimentary copies of specific displayed materials can be ordered.

The drift boat manufacturer in one state may display several models that can be purchased either for delivery right after the close of the boat show at which they are displayed or for later delivery. The manufacturer has an opportunity to get feedback from prospective customers about possible design improvements. He can also get a feel for major types of questions customers want answered and can develop interesting and effective sales messages and printed material.

**Advantages**

o   Most people attending shows are there to find out about the products or services being displayed.

o   It provides an excellent opportunity to demonstrate a product to interested people.

o   Display set-ups remain for your benefit throughout the event.

o   You can see what the competition is offering.

o   Names can be collected to add to a mailing list.

o   It is a good opportunity to get consumer feedback and product improvement ideas.

**Disadvantages**

o   Competitors can see what you are offering.

o   It may attract a lot of lookers depending on how well the occasion was advertised.

o   Organizers may be more interested in selling space than getting the kind of people to attend the event in the numbers that will produce the best results.

o   Customers may want to bargain or negotiate more with many choices available.

---

**Q5-22  What trade shows, seminars, fairs, demonstrations, or meetings might be beneficial for either display or attendance?**

**What are the major advantages of attending?**

---

## Personal Selling and Word-of-Mouth Advertising

Personal selling is especially useful as a tool to cater to the particular individual's needs and problems. If the salesperson has well-developed product knowledge or can easily explain how a particular service will benefit a particular situation, the purchase is made with greater ease and confidence. Many businesses rely heavily on personal selling as a large part of the marketing strategy, and many small businesses emphasize effective personal selling. For example, they utilize company sales representatives and point-of-purchase sales people to identify potential customers and act as consultants in satisfying particular client needs. It is what often distinguishes them from other (especially larger) competitors. The salesperson is in a position to make or break the potential sale using knowledge of the product, an ability to "read" the customer's needs, and a manner of selling that is effective both in terms of putting the customer at ease and in closing the sale.

Effective personal selling can be an important influence in the purchase decision for convenience goods, impulse items, and services (fast foods, groceries, beverages). It is often a major factor in influencing the purchase of **shopping, specialty, and industrial goods and services** where individuals are interested in the product or service but not knowledgeable enough about **your** offering. Salespeople who know a lot about the product or service (through sales meetings, seminars, conventions, on-the-job sales training), knowledgeable about people, and can effectively demonstrate the product are a real asset. They can not only help make this particular sale, they also add to a positive company image.

Effective personal selling has the distinct advantage of providing immediate feedback from the customer when the purchase is made. On-the-spot market research is available through good customer relations and effective personal selling. It offers a continual flow of valuable information to improve sales training, image development, and the particular words and images used in other advertising media.

Knowledgeable sales personnel generate more trust and confidence from their customers. Knowledge will help project a desirable image of your company when it comes time for repeat buying. For many types of products and services (life insurance, clothing, computers), sales representatives are the point of contact that clients or customers seek when they are in the market to repurchase. A good salesperson is in the position to make suggestions of product and service benefits that the customer may be unaware of (no matter how much advertising and sales promotion you may have done). Suggestions from sales personnel (who perhaps know their customers by name) give the customer a sense of personal attention in a fast-paced world. Salespeople should be trained to **listen, observe,** and **assist/consult** the customer in the buying decision. Their insights and product or service knowledge (including the ads, coupons, or special offers that are currently being advertised and promoted) can greatly affect sales.

## Advantages

o   Effective personal selling and word-of-mouth advertising can greatly increase sales, especially for a service business. It requires very little additional promotional cost such as sales meetings, commissions, bonuses, seminars, and training.

o   Sales people can explain product or service benefits in a professional, consultive manner which caters to potential customers' individual needs while making them feel important.

o   One-on-one communication between buyer and seller can help overcome any doubts, questions, or objections the potential customer may have.

o   Personal selling is especially beneficial for promoting services and goods which need special explanation, installation, customization, or trade-ins.

o   The salesperson can utilize effective personal selling skills before, during and after the actual sale. This can help reinforce overall company image, repeat sales, and good word-of-mouth advertising.

o   Personal selling can help make the intangible benefits seem more tangible as an incentive to purchase—NOW.

**Disadvantages**

o   Just as personal selling can influence sales in a positive way, sales personnel who are not informed or who don't know how to present the product or close a sale can negatively affect your sales potential.

o   No matter how much advertising and public relations has been done, effective personal selling may be necessary to support the promised and proclaimed benefits.

o   If personal selling represents a large part of the marketing efforts, sales personnel need to be able to handle customer complaints, as well as sales, in order to maintain good customer relations.

o   With the advent of mass media advertising and self-service marketing, personal selling may become less necessary for many different kinds of products—and even some services.

Q5-23 Describe how personal selling is currently utilized as a marketing tool. What are its advantages for your organization?

What would you describe as your basic sales training or personal sales approach?

A successful sales call requires a great deal of preparation. This translates into knowing all you can about your prospects.

Q5-24  Who is the real decisionmaker?

Who or what circumstances might influence the final decision?

Is this type of purchase usually a group (family or committee) decision?

What external influences may be operating? (advisors, board of directors, local economy, competition, attorneys?)

Q5-25  To improve your sales presentation, what would be useful information to know about your: (Refer to Q2-30, Worksheet 8)

Prospect?

Product or service?

Competition?

Industry trends?

## Selling Services: A Special Case

Marketing a service means marketing an intangible. Service is sold according to promises and expectations made. Word-of-mouth and effective personal sales efforts are essential ingredients for marketing almost any service.

A service business may attract customers primarily from a local area. The *Yellow Pages* or a descriptive business card, flyer, or brochure to market services may be needed. Provide a means of personal identification with your service—a unique motto, a captive logo. It will help attract and keep loyal customers. Of course, provide the quality of service expected, too.

To sell a service, sell it with confidence and tact. It often requires a more certain, yet subtle approach to your potential customer. If a client can be made to feel comfortable purchasing your services, and is satisfied with the results he or she was led to expect, you have a satisfied customer. In addition, the customer will be a good source of testimonials to help encourage repeat buying and word-of-mouth advertising among friends and associates.

Word-of-mouth advertising is its own form of personal selling and can help relieve any uncertainty before purchasing the service. Even if you only use referrals and storefront or office signage to attract customers, good word-of-mouth advertising can mean the difference between mediocre sales and a growing clientele. This type of personal selling should stress:

o   Where and when the service is available.

o   What specific or special services are provided, the quality of performance to be expected, guarantees, and how the results of using the service will directly benefit potential customers.

---

Q5-26 How do you use word-of-mouth advertising? What could be done to encourage more word-of-mouth advertising?

---

**Worksheet 14 Sales Call Planning Guide**

_____

                              Date
_____

Company                       Type of business


_____

Address                       Phone



_____

Key contact                   Position

                              Referred by

_____

Key decisionmaker?            Position


_____

If the key contact is not the decisionmaker, how best can the key contact be utilized?




_____

Potential needs of customer: (Q2-1 to 16)





_____

The decisionmaking process is described as follows:





_____

How can I help this prospect better than other competitors? (Worksheet 5)





_____

Objectives of this sales call or presentation?

Possible objections (Worksheet 2)     Possible responses   (Worksheets 11 - 13)

Supporting documentation displays, materials, people needed on call:
   (Worksheets 11 - 13, Q5-23 to 25)

Follow-up required—actions and times:

# Chapter 6
# Designing a Successful Marketing Campaign

The marketing and advertising strategies you choose can greatly affect potential sales. Advertising can promote both the overall business image and the benefits of using specific products and services. Depending on what your personal, business, and sales objectives are, the right marketing strategy can help achieve the goals in an affordable fashion. Although advertising and sales promotion are a completely controllable expense, they should really be viewed as an investment in the future of the business.

The media and means you pick must be consistent with the target market image that develops for the business and its products and services. Advertising on a classical music station would not reach the market if the target is the fashion-conscious teenager (unless listening to classical music is an "in" thing to do). Everything you, employees, sales representatives, suppliers and customers say about the product through word-of-mouth advertising can affect sales, so it is essential that time and money is spent creating the best image. Packaging and promotion, in turn, are based on that image. **You only have one chance to create a good first impression, so the way sales personnel dress and approach the customer, their sales training and knowledge, the type of media selected, and the particulars of the advertising message all contribute to the overall market image.**

You not only want to get people to buy NOW, you also want them to say a good word about the product or service to their friends, relatives, neighbors, and business associates (word-of-mouth advertising). If they often purchase intangible goods and services, a good deal of advertising and sales promotion may be needed to introduce them to new products and keep them aware of the benefits they are receiving when they use the product or service.

Once the target market groups have been identified, along with what to advertise, what total image package to create, and what media are available, the most appropriate promotional methods must be determined. This is not always an easy task, for there is a great deal of variety in the approaches a business person can take in developing the promotional mix. But the options must be studied and selections made before budgets, or any other part of the marketing campaign, can be drawn up.

Factors that will influence media selection include the cost-per-thousand reached, the amount of the advertising budget, the relative cost of various items within the budget, timing, and degree of sophistication required by the advertising and sales promotion campaign. In addition, your personal, business, and sales objectives should be considered. Select media that help distinguish the product or service and support the overall business image.

**Worksheet 15 Selecting Appropriate Advertising Media**

Identify the forms of media that seem most appropriate for the business.

| Medium | Major Benefit in Use |
|---|---|
| **Television (Q5-3, 4)** | |
| Which channels? | Frequency? |
| | |
| **Radio (Q5-5, 6 Worksheet 12)** | |
| Which stations? | Frequency? |
| | |
| **Newspapers (Q5-7, 8)** | |
| Which ones? | Sections? |
| | |
| **Magazines (Q5-9, 10)** | |
| Which ones? | Sections? |
| | |
| **Yellow Pages (Q5-12)** | Sections? |

Printed promotional materials and direct mail (Q5-1, 17, 18)
(Check those that apply)

__ Letterheads/envelopes
__ Flyers/brochures
__ Business forms
__ Informational pamphlets
__ Catalogs
__ Special announcements
__ Seasonal sales
__ Grand openings
__ Product specification sheets
__ Mailing lists
__ Direct-mail materials (list)

__ _____

__ _____

__ Invitations
__ Appointment cards
__ Coupons
__ Gift certificates
__ Thank-you notes/cards
__ Registration forms
__ Newsletter
__ Evaluation forms
__ Market research questionnaires
__ Special one-time-only offers

__ _____

__ _____

Signs and displays (Q5-13 to 16)

__ Billboards
__ Reader boards
__ Point-of purchase displays
__ Floor displays
__ Product demonstrations

__ Exhibits/trade show displays
__ Posters
__ In-house product information racks
__ Taxis
__ Bus and other transit advertising

Special promotional events (Q5-18 to 21)

__ Special clearance sales
__ Awards and prizes
__ Contests
__ Parades

__ Arts and crafts festivals
__ Sidewalk sales
__ Grand openings
__ Open houses

Public relations and publicity (Q5-19 to 21)

__ News releases
__ Press conferences
__ Business or personal profiles

__ Feature articles
__ Interviews (radio and television)
__ Photographs

Personal selling (Q5-22 to 26)

__ Business cards
__ Personal contact
__ Sales training

__ Telephone contact
__ Product or service referrals
__ Sales approach

Once you have an idea which are the most appropriate advertising and sales promotion techniques for your product or service, compare their market coverage, target audience reached, costs in terms of time and advertising space purchased and the specific benefits derived from their use. Weigh the costs and benefits associated with utilizing various media in terms of the overall promotional mix, advertising budget, and the image desired for the products or services.

The Advertising Media Comparison Chart* is designed to aid in developing the media comparison summary of Worksheet 16.

*Reprinted with permission of Bank of America, N.T. & S.A., *Small Business Reporter,* "Advertising Small Business," Vol. 13, No. 8. Copyright 1976, 1978.

## Advertising Media Comparison Chart

| Medium | Market Coverage | Type of Audience | Sample Time/Space Costs |
|---|---|---|---|
| DAILY NEWSPAPER | Single community or entire metro area; zoned editions sometimes available. | General. Tends more toward older age group, slightly higher income and education. | Per agate line weekday<br>Circ: 7,000 $ .25<br>16,500 $ .35<br>21,300 $ .60<br>219,200 $ 2.102. |
| WEEKLY NEWSPAPER | Single community usually; sometimes a metro area. | General; usually resident of a smaller community. | Per agate line:<br>Circ: 5,400 $ .35<br>20,900 $ .55<br>40,000 $ 1.20 |
| SHOPPER | Most households in a single community; chain shoppers can cover a metro area. | Consumer households. | One quarter page, black and white; open rate<br>13,000 $ 45.00<br>22,500 $185.00<br>183,400 $760.00 |
| TELEPHONE DIREC- TORIES | Geographic area or occupational field served by the directory. | Active shoppers for goods or services. | Yellow Pages per half-column per month<br>10-49,000 $ 35.00<br>100-249,000 $ 63.00<br>500-999,000 $152.00 |
| DIRECT MAIL | Controlled by the advertiser. | Controlled by the advertiser through use of demographic lists. | Production and mailing cost of an 8 1/2 x 11" 4-color brochure; order card & reply env. label addressed; third class mail: $.35 each in quantities of 50,000 |
| RADIO | Definable market area surrounding the station's location. | Selected audiences provided by stations with distinct programming formats. | Per 60-second drive-time spot: one time<br>Pop: 400,000 $ 45.00<br>1,100,000 $ 115.00<br>3,500,000 $200.00<br>13,000,000 $385.00 |
| TELEVISION | Definable market area surrounding the station's location. | Varies with the time of day; tends toward younger age group, less print-oriented. | Per 30-second daytime spot; non-preemptible status<br>Pop: 400,000 $125.00<br>1,100,000 $370.00<br>3,500,000 $615.00<br>13,000,000 $740.00 |

| Particular Suitability | Major Advantage | Major Disadvantage |
|---|---|---|
| All general retailers. | Flexibility. | Nonselective audience. |
| Retailers who service a strictly local market. | Local identification. | Limited readership. |
| Neighborhood retailers and service businesses. | Consumer orientation. | A giveaway and not always read. |
| Services, retailers of brand-name items; highly specialized retailers. | Users are in the market for goods or services. | Limited to active shoppers. |
| New and expanding businesses; those using coupon returns or catalogs. | Personalized approach to an audience of good prospects. | High CPM. |
| Business catering to identifiable groups: teens, commuters, housewives. | Market selectivity wide market coverage. | Must be bought consistently to be of value. |
| Sellers of products or services with wide appeal | Dramatic impact, market selectivity, wide market coverage. | High cost of time and production. |

| Medium | Market Coverage | Type of Audience | Sample Time/Space Costs |
|---|---|---|---|
| TRANSIT | Urban or metro community served by transit system; may be limited to a few transit | Transit riders, especially wage earners and shoppers; pedestrians. | Per 11" x 28" card: per month:<br>1 bus   $ 5.00<br>500 buses   $2,500.00<br>Per 30" x 144" posters per month:<br>1 bus   $ 85.00<br>170 buss   $14,110.00 |
| OUTDOOR | Entire metro area or single neigh-borhood. | General, especially auto drivers. | Per 12 x 25-ft poster, 100 GRP per month<br>Pop: 17,900   $650.00<br>(5 posters)<br>484,900   $9,770.00<br>(54 posters)<br>10,529,300   162,400.00<br>(500 posters) |
| LOCAL MAGAZINE | Entire metro area or region; zoned editions some-times available. | General; tends toward better educated, more affluent. | Per one-sixth page, black and white; open rate:<br>Circ: 30,000   $285.00<br>43,750   $435.00<br>163,460   $770.00 |

Reprinted with permission from Bank of America, NT&SA, "Advertising Small Business," *Small Business Reporter,* copyright 1982.

| Particular Suitability | Major Advantage | Major Disadvantage |
|---|---|---|
| Businesses along transit routes, especially those appealing to wage earners. | Repetition and length of exposure. | Limited audience. |
| Amusements, tourist businesses, brand-name retailers. | Dominant size, frequency of exposure. | Clutter of many signs reduces effectiveness of each one. |
| Restaurants, entertainments, specialty shops, mail-order businesses. | Delivery of a loyal special interest audience. | Limited audience. |

**Worksheet 16   Media Evaluation and Comparison Summary**

| Medium | Circulation | Audience Type | Cost per ad | Cost per 1000 | Frequency of ad | Expected Response Rate |
|---|---|---|---|---|---|---|
| | | | | | | |
| | | | | | | |
| | | | | | | |
| | | | | | | |
| | | | | | | |
| | | | | | | |
| | | | | | | |
| | | | | | | |
| | | | | | | |
| | | | | | | |
| | | | | | | |
| | | | | | | |
| | | | | | | |
| | | | | | | |
| | | | | | | |
| | | | | | | |
| | | | | | | |
| | | | | | | |

## Developing Your Advertising Budget

The amount of advertising dollars needed to communicate awareness resulting in sales will depend on many factors such as:

o   How much there is to allocate for advertising and sales promotion.

o   How successful you were last year in promotional efforts.

o   What competitors are doing—how much they're spending and on which media alternatives.

o   What similar businesses are spending as a ballpark comparison or rule of thumb.

o   The stage in the product's life cycle.

o   Which products or services should be emphasized next year (sell out discontinued product lines, promote new fall fashions).

o   Changes in the economic, social, political, demographic, and psychological profile of the target customers.

o   Location of the business outlet or office (the farther away from target customers, the more it may cost to advertise a location)

o   Intuitive feeling given the influences mentioned above.

o   The overall **audience reached, ad frequency** necessary to maintain awareness, and the **degree of continuity** needed to remain consistent with the total image package. (For many products the customer must see the message several times before it will lead to a purchase.)

o   The goals associated with the advertising campaign (increasing sales by a certain percent, introducing a new product or service, or maintaining good customer relations).

o   Whether manufacturers are willing to provide cooperative advertising money to help stretch a promotional budget.

o   Whether to hire an advertising agency or media consultant.

---

Q6-1 List the relevant cost factors affecting your advertising budget.

---

Q6-2 How much was spent last year and the year before?

As a percentage of sales last year, how much was budgeted or spent for advertising?

The year before?

**Industry guideline percentages** are published in government reports (check the Internal Revenue Service and the Census report) and financial institutions, such as Dun & Bradstreet, Robert Morris Associates reports, and the Accounting Corporation of America. Most of these are available through your public library or through libraries of media specialists from whom you purchase time and space, or media consultants and advertising agencies that help design your marketing campaign.

Q6-3 What are the industry averages for advertising and promotion for your type of business?

For many small and large businesses alike, the **amount that competition** spends on yearly advertising and sales promotion may be the impetus for your budget decisions and media selections. If you are in a highly competitive market or are promoting commonly purchased goods and services, a good strategy for distinguishing your product or service is needed. If you can't **at least meet or exceed the competition** in terms of media strategy and dollars spent (for example, the corner grocery compared with large national chain stores), then you need to select media that are unlike those of your competitors (well-designed window displays, point-of-purchase free samples) to help distinguish the product or service.

Q6-4 Which media are unlike the competitors' and therefore might be wisely utilized?

When introducing a new product or service to the marketplace, use more **intuition** (along with **industry guidelines**, if they are available) in determining the right amount to budget and the most advantageous media selection strategy. Estimate the amount you feel necessary or affordable and then allocate those advertising dollars so that the greatest amount is spent in the first two to six months of creating awareness of the new product or service.

It may make good sense in launching a new product or service (especially a new business) to determine the promotional budget according to whatever **residual funds** are available after all other projected expenses are taken into account. This method is often dangerous, however, since not spending enough promotional dollars to effectively reach the target customers can defeat any sales potential. **Promotion is an investment in helping to materialize sales potential.** Careful monitoring month-by-month of how actual sales match projected sales will help guide you in determining the promotional budget and media strategy necessary to develop essential customer awareness.

The most easily adaptable and most commonly used method of determining the total advertising and sales promotion budget for the coming year is to apply a certain **percentage of sales** (either to last year's sales, if you were in business, or to expected sales for this coming year). This method is easy to calculate and realistic in approach. It is possible to adjust the percentage according to whether the objective is to increase market share or to change the emphasis from advertising to personal selling. If the goal is to change company image it may reduce the percentage applied to sales. This method makes budget decisions easy, flexible, and reasonable to calculate.

Q6-5 What percent of sales do you expect to spend on advertising next year? (Refer to Worksheet 7.)

One variation of the above method is to **develop a fixed percentage per unit sold** and apply it to projected sales. Determine how many advertising dollars are necessary to create one sale, then develop a percentage which can be applied to overall expected sales for the upcoming year. This method is appropriate for large, expensive shopping and specialty goods (like furs, cars, houses, high fashion jewelry) and services (like computer engineering and program design, interior decorating, and investment specialists).

Whether introducing a totally new product or service, adding another to an existing line, moving a store or office location, clearing out old merchandise, or changing the business environment, it will be possible to utilize a combination of the above methods. While creating a budget, consider the following profit planners.

o   Stores in less favorable locations need to budget more advertising in order to attract potential customers—so do stores that are new or expanding.

o   Service providers should emphasize availability and image to attract clients.

o   Strong competition in the marketplace increases the budget necessary to attract customers from competitors.

o   Stores and service outlets which emphasize lower prices as a major benefit tend to promote more heavily than businesses emphasizing other benefits.

o   Special dates and events that offer additional sales opportunities need advance budget planning (for example, payroll days of important local businesses, heavy store traffic days, local night openings, tie-ins with national and local merchandising events, new or expanding departments, and inventory reductions at year's end).

o   Take advantage of any cooperative advertising dollars available for your products.

o   Stretch the advertising budget by converting a specific ad in a newspaper or magazine to a direct mail or publicity piece by having it reproduced and mailed (to customer lists or media publicists). Whatever you've already paid for ad layout, photos, design, and art renderings can be reused for a different target audience with little or no additional cost.

o   Advertising and promotional efforts can often become more effective when they are implemented by professionals such as advertising agents and media consultants.

o   Take advantage of local media representatives (especially newspapers, magazines, and television) to get **free** advice and assistance in preparing ad copy, design, layout, and correct media timing.

o   Trade associations, the Better Business Bureau, Chamber of Commerce, and networking organizations are valuable sources of information and assistance when determining an appropriate advertising budget.

o   When planning to develop an organization, add specialists in graphic design, artwork, and ad layout to your list of experts. Printers and direct-mail list brokers can also be helpful with suggestions to stretch advertising efforts.

o   Be aware of industry guidelines both for typical ad budget as percent of sales and usual media selected. For example, mail-order firms' ad budgets may vary from 18% to 30% of sales while using direct mail, magazines, and television. Auto supply shops may have a typical ad budget closer to 1% to 2% and use direct mail, flyers, newspapers, and *Yellow Pages*.

## Cooperative Advertising

If you have a retail outlet through which products manufactured by others are sold, or a service organization that carries related products (such as a cleaning establishment which has rug shampoo products), it is possible to stretch advertising dollars by cooperating with product manufacturers in running specific ads which are mutually advantageous. The retail outlet or service organization can get advertising expenses reimbursed (often up to 50%) by specifying the manufacturer's logo, product, or product line in their advertising.

This form of advertising is often overlooked by small businesses because there is always extra paperwork involved—retailers must meet manufacturers' requirements in order to get reimbursed. Usually there is a requirement to keep detailed records and send in copies of advertisements (tearsheets) to get reimbursed. Although this may seem like a hassle for a small business owner with little spare time for paperwork, co-op dollars from supplier sources can boost your promotional effort by as much as 300%! Almost every manufacturer and supplier offers some type of cooperative advertising and free promotional brochures.

Even the smallest retail outlets and service organizations that use manufactured products can benefit. Retailers usually get a better price than manufacturers when buying advertising space and time (media discounts), so it becomes profitable for the manufacturer to invest cooperative advertising dollars for their products that you sell. Manufacturers will also offer cooperative advertising to retailers as an incentive to start carrying their products. If the product does well, both manufacturer and retailer benefit.

Although arrangements vary, most reimbursements are based on either a percentage of volume the dealer does with the manufacturer or a per-unit allowance on sales made during a specified time period. Since manufacturers who offer cooperative advertising arrangements include the cost in determining the price, at least check into the possibilities (otherwise your potential reimbursement becomes more profit for the manufacturer). Of course, you may find that cooperative advertising is not cost-effective given the manufacturer's requirements.

If you manufacture a product and seek distributors, dealers, and retail outlets, consider cooperative advertising arrangements as incentives. This is essentially a form of sales promotion. It helps stretch advertising dollars in creating outlets and awareness of your product, which of course can improve your profit. Although it may be useful to compare industry standards (and collect examples that you see of cooperative advertising arrangements), it may be best to develop different requirements. Such requirements may include the use of a logo together with the product name, other limits on the dealer when showing competitive products, or proof that the dealer has actually run the ad in order to qualify for expense reimbursement. There is a great deal of flexibility in structuring cooperative advertising arrangements, although the the Federal Trade Commission does prescribe some requirements.

---

Q6-6 Describe cooperative advertising possibilities or requirements.

---

## Advertising Agencies and Media Consultants

If you have a $5,000 annual advertising budget, should you hire an advertising agency? Probably not. Why not? Most agencies operate on a commission of 15% of what is paid to the media. Charges for out-of-pocket expenses, such as artwork or photography, are also passed on to the client. The agency has to cover direct and indirect costs and make a profit. If the average monthly advertising budget runs about $400 ($5,000 ÷ 12 = $417), the agency's commission is $62.50. It may be possible to find a new, small, hungry firm that would be interested, or one with a set fee or fee/commission combination that could be approached. If it is possible to budget $10-15,000 per month in advertising, many agencies will be interested. Finding an ad agency is like getting a loan from a bank: the larger the loan the greater the likelihood of getting it.

**Worksheet 17 Advertising Budget Worksheet**

How much did you spend last year on advertising? _____

   As a percent of sales (Q6-2, 5) _____ %

   Were you satisfied with the return on advertising expenses?

   What way do you have of measuring effectiveness of your advertising? (Q6-7)

_____

Do your major competitors spend more or less than you do on advertising? (Q6-1, 3, 4)

_____

My product or service is in which life-cycle stage? (Q1-14)

_____

The location of my kind of business is excellent, good, fair, or poor. (Worksheet 4)

_____

My sales goals for next year are what percentage of last year? _____ %

This translates to a goal of $_____ (Q4-1, Worksheet 7)

_____

Using national percentage of sales figures for your industry, how much would you budget for next year's advertising? (Q6-2, 3)

   Is there a fixed amount allocated to advertising each month? (Q6-3, 5)

   List positive or negative social, political, demographic, economic, or legal factors that might affect sales next year. (Q2-2, 30, Q3-5, 6)

_____

Gut feel—The total minimum budget for advertising this next year: (Q6-1 to 5)

_____

Based on all the above indicators, next year's advertising budget will need to be:

   $_____ next year or an average of $_____/month

   in order to reach my sales goal. (Q4-1, Worksheet 7)

_____

On the other hand, even with a small budget it may be wise to use an agency. Burton Baskin and Irvine Robbins approached a small new ad agency with all of $500. It was just after World War II. Baskin and Robbins had started an ice cream business, and two or three small stores were selling their ice cream to retail customers. A large dairy firm tried to stop the stores from carrying Baskin and Robbins ice cream. The fledgling Carson-Roberts agency helped them out in the interest of possibly getting a long-term client relationship. They recommended the expenditure of the $500 on a fun image: painting pink and chocolate colored balloons on a white background on the delivery trucks and stationery and emphasizing lots of flavors from which to choose. Not bad advice—and the agency grew with its client!

Advertising agencies can help you by selecting the appropriate media and by creating ideas for promoting the business, product, or service. They can also provide technical expertise by writing copy and designing art work. Some agencies will help with marketing research and promotion. The usual advice is to shop around. Fees or commissions can usually be negotiated.

---

Q6-7 Marketing areas in which an advertising agency might be helpful:



---

Advertising agencies and independent media consultants are in business to provide a service which involves creating awareness of your product or service. They may be a full-service agency with the talent available to create a total image package—the logo, package design, motto, benefits, photos, film, sound effects, commercial production, layout ad message and image design to acting as your publicity or public relations agent. They can create press releases and help develop other effective forms of sales promotions materials and creative ideas. On the other hand, some of that talent may be available within your circle of associates, family, and friends. You may need only to hire specialists who consult on one major aspect (such as a photo layout expert, publicity agent, graphic artist, designer, or printer) for an overall marketing campaign.

If you want to hire someone outside of the organization to assist in marketing the products or services, weigh the cost of their combined talent against the expected results. Agencies derive their income from charging the client or account a flat fee or hourly rate for services or expenses plus a fixed percent. However, they get the majority of their income from media commissions (usually 15% on the cost of time and space purchased through their agency).

For specialized help, or if a relatively small advertising budget is available, media consultants and smaller agencies will be more likely to want your account. Large agencies prefer large accounts that have budgets to match, whereas one person or small agencies are much more willing to cater to individual needs on a smaller budget. Fees are negotiable, so be sure to ask questions and compare several agencies.

In any case, work with someone who has a good feel for the product or service and can create the desired results at a reasonable cost. Likewise, your account must become profitable for the agency or consultant to provide the service you desire and expect. Good communication and feedback are essential for effective use of outside media. Finding the right agent, and the agent's follow-up to ensure that ads placed are reaching the most appropriate target customers, can help assure a successful relationship. But the overall responsibility remains with you to communicate to the agent the image you want.

Q6-8 List some agencies/consultants you may want to use:

## Sales Forecasting

As can be seen from reading the previous sections, the annual advertising and promotional budget is closely linked to sales goals for the upcoming year. Sales goals, in turn, are affected by personal and overall organizational goals, the availability of competing products and services, the relative newness of the product or service, and many other factors. Complete the following worksheet to clarify sales objectives that can be achieved through good marketing strategy.

Developing an effective media strategy and sufficient budget to accomplish this coming year's sales goals is the purpose of any media plan. Understanding and clarifying your current marketing objectives and proposed media strategy can help you develop a marketing plan that can serve as a yardstick for assessing future marketing strategy. Answer the questions in Worksheet 19 as specifically as possible before outlining specific media strategy and budget on Worksheet 20.

**Worksheet 18   Sales and Marketing Goals**

What results do I expect to achieve through my marketing strategy? Write a brief statement in each of these strategic planning areas. This should provide a roadmap for planning sales, pricing, advertising and sales promotion activities. (Refer to Worksheets 6, 7, 17)

**Overall business image:** I would like to develop an image whereby my potential customers perceive me, my business, and the products or services I offer as: (Worksheets 5, 10, Q2-3 to 6)

**Yearly sales:** I would like to increase my current sales by _____ percent or $_____ within the next six months to one year. (Q4-1)

**Market share:** I would like to increase my market share in relation the competition by _____ percent during the next six months to one year. (Q4-1)

**Market penetration:** I would like to bring increased awareness about my product or service to at least _____ new customers through my marketing strategy.

**Growth:** I would like to experience growth in my business as evidenced by: (Q4-1)

**Product or Service Diversification:** I would like to be able to offer _____ new products or services that are related/unrelated to current offerings.

**Profit:** I would like my advertising budget to generate enough sales to afford me an after-tax profit of $_____, which is _____ percent above last year. (Worksheet 7)

## Worksheet 19 Marketing Strategy and Budget Review

Are you satisfied with the overall market image of the company and individual products or services? If no, how would you specifically change the total image packaging? (Q4-5, 17, Worksheet 5, 10).

_____

How long has your product or service been available in the marketplace? (Q1-14)

_____

At what stage in the product life cycle is it? (Q1-14)

_____

The location of the business requires _____ more or _____ less advertising than that required by competitors. (Worksheets 4 and 5)

List any factors in the marketplace that might affect sales this coming year: (Q4-3 to 7)

|  | Positive effect | Negative effect |
|---|---|---|
| Social |  |  |
| Political |  |  |
| Demographic |  |  |
| Economic |  |  |
| Legal |  |  |
| Psychological |  |  |
| Other factors |  |  |

My sales goals for this year are _____ percent of last year's sales. (See Worksheet 18, Q4-1)

My initial feeling is that the total minimum budget for advertising and sales promotional efforts this coming year should be $_____, which I've determined by the following method: (See Worksheet 17)

How much did you budget **last year** or intend to budget **this coming year** (See Worksheets 16 and 17) for:

**Advertising**

Television $_____

Radio        $_____

   Which stations? _____

   Times? _____

Newspapers $_____

   Which papers? _____

   Sections? _____

   Classified ads? _____    Display ads? _____

Magazines   $_____

   Which ones _____

   Sections? _____

Yellow Pages $_____

   Display ad?_____

   Headings_____

**Printed promotional materials**

Direct mail              $_____

Letterhead/envelopes     $_____

Catalogs                 $_____

Flyers/Brochures         $_____

Special sales            $_____

**Other sales promotions**

Signs and displays $_____

Special promotional events

      $_____/event

Public relations $_____

Publicity $_____

Sales training $_____

Sales incentives $_____

What objective measures and criteria have you established for determining the effectiveness of your media strategy and budget? (Q6-8, Worksheets 16, 17)

Cost-per-thousand reached? _____

Return on investment in advertising? _____

Coupon percentage returned? _____

Marketing research questionnaires? _____

Other criteria? _____

Were you satisfied with the effectiveness (the dollar return, image created, market share or penetration) achieved through your promotional strategy last year? _____ If not, explain how you intend to change it. (Q5-1, 2, Worksheet 18)

_____

Are you satisfied with your current pricing strategy? (Q3-11, Worksheet 8)

If not, explain how you would change it this coming year.

_____

Who are your major competitors and what are their media strategies? (Q5-2, Q3-5, and Worksheets 5 and 16)

_____

Do you intend to take advantage of any cooperative advertising arrangements available to you? (Q6-6)

_____

How much money is available to help reimburse your advertising expenses?

$_____ Special terms

_____

Did you/do you intend to utilize an advertising agency or media consultant? (Q6-7)

For what purpose?

Commission or fee basis?

_____

As you can see from the previous worksheets, sales forecasts will influence budget expenditures, as will goals, competition, media selection, and many other factors. Before finalizing this coming year's budget, **evaluate the various strategies and combinations of media and sales promotion techniques in the marketing campaign. Set performance standards** in each area of promotion to determine the effectiveness of dollars spent in each area. Also, **monitor feedback** in relation to sales and image created through advertising and promotional efforts. All these factors contribute to having an effective media plan that will be organized, yet flexible enough to help you accomplish your marketing objectives.

Before actually tackling this year's marketing plan and budget, read the following example. It describes how to develop a monthly promotional budget for a given product.

Assume that you are a new business and want to introduce a relatively new product in a specific geographic market—unique comic-book character crayons and eraser sets in the Los Angeles to San Francisco area. You have checked all the resources suggested and have a good profile in mind of the target customer groups. They are:

o    Youngsters between the ages of 5 and 11;

o    Parents and grandparents of these youngsters;

o    Schools in the community.

The initial plan is to market them locally and if they do as well as expected, to market them in other geographic regions of the United States, Japan, and eventually in Europe (within three to five years). Guidelines have been developed for the product, and estimates are that about 5% of expected sales should be spent during the first year for media advertising. The marketing thrust will include 30-second radio spots on ten stations, a direct-mail coupon campaign offering a free coloring book to anyone responding to a questionnaire, and point-of-purchase displays in toy stores, grocery stores, and school supply houses.

Using good marketing research, develop a monthly sales forecast for the next year and annual forecasts for the next three to five years. Of course, market trends and changing economic and other market environment conditions will influence future sales projections. If this is a new product, the major thrust should be in the early stages of product introduction. It's vital to advertise, NOW!

Given all the factors at hand, assume that the sales projection for the first year is $50,000. You estimate that 10% of gross sales will be spent for promo- tional efforts. That's a budget allocation of an initial $5,000. At least double the amount will be needed for this first year ($10,000) in order to even get a new product off the ground and penetrate the market in competing creative outlets for kids. Many new businesses count on spending 100% of their normal annual estimated budget as an extra effort needed to create awareness of their new product among competing products during the first four to six weeks of product introduction, with the normal amount to be spent in addition over the next 11 months. This means budgeting $10,000 for this first year for the crayon and eraser sales. For the following year the plan calls for investing 10% (as usual) of expected sales. The second year projections call for sales of $65-70,000. The budget is 10%, or $6,500 to $7,000, for the second year, and so on. Adjust the advertising percentage according to changing market factors and organizational goals. Make a yearly sales forecast and monitor it throughout the year to adjust media strategy to meet any changing conditions.

It will be helpful in determining the specific budget allocations and media and sales promotion expenditures to break sales down into monthly estimates. For example, given a first-year sales forecast of $50,000 and the need to spend 100% of the normal planned budget in the product launch period ($5,000 before the back-to-school month of September), in addition to the regular planned budget of $5,000, the budget planning sheet might initially look like this for the first year.

|  | July | August | September | October | November | December |
|---|---|---|---|---|---|---|
| Estimated gross sales | $3,000 | $2,000 | $11,500 | $1,000 | $2,500 | $22,000 |
| Budgeted (10%) | $300 | $200 | $1,150 | $100 | $250 | $2,200 |
| New product launch | $1,000 | $4,000 | -0- | -0- | -0- | -0- |

|  | January | February | March | April | May | June |
|---|---|---|---|---|---|---|
| Estimated gross sales | $2,000 | $1,000 | $1,000 | $1,000 | $1,000 | $2,000 |
| Budgeted (10%) | $200 | $100 | $100 | $100 | $100 | $200 |

The advertisements will start running about two to four weeks before each month's sales are expected. That is, don't wait until the end of August to spend the launching budget of $5,000 in advertising and sales promotion (perhaps a direct mail-order coupon special offer). Start the product launching campaign in late July and early August before school starts in September. The purpose of determining the budget is to help plan the timing of the media messages so that they will have the greatest impact on expected sales—so PLAN AHEAD!

## Yearly Sales Forecast and Marketing Budget Plan

A written marketing and budget plan will provide a detailed blueprint of how sales goals can be achieved with selected promotional efforts. Having such a plan for each product or service (or grouping of similar products and services) will help organize marketing efforts so that they can maximize the expected results. A marketing budget plan should take into account the seasonality of the business—its particular sales flow, peaks, and valleys. Be certain that timing of the advertising and sales promotion efforts are coordinated with the inventory control and sales personnel so that they are all aligned to take advantage of this ebb and flow. Hiring extra help around Christmas and for special sales, for example, can help the product's image as well as profitability.

By structuring the media plan and expenditures on advertising and sales promotions to take advantage of proper timing in the marketplace, invaluable market exposure will be gained. Once people become familiar with what you have to offer, the actual quality of the products or services, in relation to what is projected, will determine actual sales.

Remember to remain flexible with the media strategy and budget allocations, allowing adjustments to be made because of changing market conditions. Through careful monitoring of the plan you will help ensure marketing success, especially when launching a new product. Monitoring should include comparing projected to actual monthly sales and evaluating the relative effectiveness of various selected media alternatives. Don't hesitate to ask a lot of questions, gather information about potential target customers and the media that best serve them, and gather samples of competitors' advertising and sales promotion ideas for comparison purposes. Recognize investment opportunities in the areas of effective marketing, sales promotion, and media strategy.

## Worksheet 20 Yearly Sales Forecast and Marketing Budget

| | January Forecast/Actual | February Forecast/Actual | March Forecast/Actual | April Forecast/Actual | May Forecast/Actual | June Forecast/Actual |
|---|---|---|---|---|---|---|
| Gross sales | $<br>$ | $<br>$ | $<br>$ | $<br>$ | $<br>$ | $<br>$ |
| Marketing budget | $<br>$ | $<br>$ | $<br>$ | $<br>$ | $<br>$ | $<br>$ |
| Advertising | | | | | | |
| Station/times | | | | | | |
| Television (Q5-2, 3) | | | | | | |
| Radio (Q5-4, 5) | | | | | | |
| Names/sections | | | | | | |
| Newspapers (Q5-7, 8) | | | | | | |
| Magazines (Q5-9 to 11) | | | | | | |
| Yellow Pages (Q5-12) | | | | | | |
| Printed promotional materials | | | | | | |
| Direct mail (Q5-17) | | | | | | |
| Flyers/brochures | | | | | | |
| Coupons | | | | | | |
| Posters/handbills | | | | | | |
| Catalogs | | | | | | |
| Newsletter | | | | | | |
| Other printed materials | | | | | | |
| Signs and displays (Q5-13 to 15) | | | | | | |
| Billboard/transit | | | | | | |
| Point of purchase/ windows | | | | | | |
| Sales promotion (Q5-14) | | | | | | |
| Publicity and public relations (Q5-20) | | | | | | |
| Personal selling and sales training (Q5-21 to 24) | | | | | | |
| Other marketing ideas | | | | | | |

| July Forecast/Actual | August Forecast/Actual | September Forecast/Actual | October Forecast/Actual | November Forecast/Actual | December Forecast/Actual | TOTAL |
|---|---|---|---|---|---|---|
| $ | $ | $ | $ | $ | $ | $ |
| $ | $ | $ | $ | $ | $ | $ |
| | | | | | | |
| | | | | | | |
| | | | | | | |
| | | | | | | |
| | | | | | | |
| | | | | | | |
| | | | | | | |
| | | | | | | |
| | | | | | | |
| | | | | | | |
| | | | | | | |
| | | | | | | |
| | | | | | | |
| | | | | | | |
| | | | | | | |
| | | | | | | |
| | | | | | | |
| | | | | | | |
| | | | | | | |
| | | | | | | |
| | | | | | | |
| | | | | | | |
| | | | | | | |
| | | | | | | |

## Evaluating Your Marketing Plan and Yearly Budget

Overall marketing strategy and sales forecasts need to reflect good, continual research. The budget and media strategy need to be realistic in light of this research. Observations should be continually made about what's happening in the market. If marketing objectives are clearly stated (refer to Worksheets 7 and 18), it will be possible to see if the media and sales promotion strategy are accomplishing these goals. Some media effects are harder to measure than others. Some (like public relations and publicity) are intended more for goodwill and a positive image than directly related to sales. When evaluating the current marketing plan, consider the long-run as well as short-run marketing strategy for promoting the products and services.

It is helpful to review the budget periodically (every three to six months at least) as you continue to update market information (review your Sales Forecasting and Budgeting Worksheets 15 to 20). Remember the following pointers for measuring customer response to media, its message, sales promotions, sales presentations, and publicity:

o   Utilizing coupons in newspaper and magazine ads, as well as in direct-mail campaigns, is an excellent method for comparing audience reached to sales response.

o   Keeping a file on ads—yours and competitors' ads—helps keep track of which ads best attract customers. Which pictures, which benefits, which copy message and layout work best?

o   Using an on-the-spot survey to ask customers and passers-by what they think, prefer, buy, like the most, or need can develop sales potential.

o   Sometimes concentration on one major medium will affect sales better than just one spot ad in each of several media types, so it may be worthwhile to repeat the same ad layout rather than continually create new ads.

o   For service businesses especially, ask who referred a potential client and follow up on how many sales result from word-of-mouth advertising.

o   Provide a free gift, sample, or hidden message in your advertising as an incentive to respond—a good way to observe the same ad in different media.

Q6-9 Describe how you will evaluate media effectiveness.

# Chapter 7
# Delivering Customer Satisfaction

The best advertisements in the world will only bring customers to your door. You must **keep** them, once they arrive, by bringing them satisfaction—without that, no business has a future. Satisfying the customer is the capstone to any marketing plan.

The period of time during which the customer is making the "I am going to purchase this item" decision offers many **opportunities**. The customer is deciding what and how much to buy at what price. The customer is forming impressions and developing attitudes toward the business. These impressions and attitudes affect what the customer will say about the product or service to others, whether or not the customer will buy again, and if the product or service is liked.

By this stage, the potential client or customer has heard about the product or service. Maybe an ad caught their attention. You offered a free seminar with wine and cheese to explain your product. The service was written up in the public interest section of a newspaper. Direct-mail coupons good for a free cup of coffee were sent to browsers. An open house was advertised. A free demonstration was given at home.

## Initiating the Sale

Remember that the objective is to make sales by having **satisfied customers**. A satisfied customer will have a good attitude toward the product. A satisfied customer will tell others and will lead to additional sales.

> Q7-1 How easy is it for the customer to decide and to order?
>
>
>
> Can the place of business be found easily?

**Example**

> One nursery was located in a difficult place to find. The nursery included a map in every ad. Customers were rewarded for finding the nursery. There were signs at the business thanking the customers for going to the trouble to find it. The signs also assured the customers that this distant location allowed the nursery to offer lower prices due to lower overhead. The nursery capitalized on the location. It risked getting fewer new customers by using the ad space for a map rather than copy. It paid off in customers who were able to find the place.

o Deciding and ordering should be as close together as possible.

It makes no sense to spend $600 on a television ad that offers, "Call this minute to get your reduced rates" without being able to take the calls. But consider a cable television firm that does a lot of advertising for its services. Each ad says to call a certain number. If you call the numbers noted for subscriptions, billing, repair, the numbers are normally busy for hours on end; if you can get through, a hold system then kicks you in to a person within about five to seven minutes. Dealing with them by mail is a lost cause as mail responses are handled by a different operation. If you order increased service by mail, it would not occur for at least two months, whereas a phone order is handled within a couple of days. This firm will survive as long as it has no competition. If a customer cannot decide and order in a timely fashion, there will be no sale.

o First impressions are important. By the time the prospect gets physically close enough to make the decision to buy, calls to place an order, or writes a check, an impression has already been formed. The client has a preconceived notion what the product or service is or looks like. This step adds to that first impression—it confirms or changes it.

---

Q7-2 What first impression does your product or service give?

---

o Real estate agents are aware of the significance of the first sight impression. "Curb appeal" is stressed. The lawn is cut, trees and shrubs are pruned, amd the outside of the house is freshly painted.

o Free seminars where you will find out about a tax shelter or how to make a fortune in the stock market are staffed by professionally attired people. Your name is taken. You are made welcome. The presentation is in color with tastefully presented pictures or script. As your comfort level increases, your feelings of trust for this group increase.

o In a retail operation, the salespeople are an important part of this impression. People want to be helped to find what they are after. They don't want to wait once they have decided to buy. Like it or not, a customer finds it difficult to separate the attitudes toward the salesperson from the attitudes formed toward the product or service. Inappropriately dressed salespeople can be a problem.

o There is a wide range of sins which the consumer will neither forget nor forgive. Some may be unique to your business. How can you sensitize yourself and your employees to those things which impress customers favorably and those which give a negative impression?

**Example: Consumer diary approach**

Put yourself in the place of the consumer. For one week, propose to the employees (if you have them) that everyone keep consumer diaries which will be discussed on Friday after work over a cup of coffee.

The object of this exercise is to get yourselves into a **consumer-oriented** frame of mind. Record each consumer experience. Then act as a consultant to the owner of the business involved. This is an on-paper activity. When everyone gets together, each can read worst and best examples. Get into the habit of looking for practices which make a positive impression on the consumer as well as those which make a negative impression. As you discuss this exercise, it may become all too clear that the majority of the experiences recorded will be negative.

## Delivery of the Product, Production of the Service

After the purchase is made is a critical opportunity to win a satisfied consumer or close a sale. Several examples follow showing ways to win a satisfied customer at the moment of delivery of the product or service.

You've just been handed the money or the contract has been signed. The client needs **reassurance** that this was a wise decision. There is a moment:" "omigosh— did I make the right decision?" At that instant is the "Thank you for your purchase. I'm certain that you will get many years of carefree service from XYZ. We've had excellent feedback on it."

You've just chopped three inches off the youngster's hair. Up comes the mirror. "That really shows off your fine features." Give assurance. Refrain from "Finally, your brother will be able to recognize you!" Make it a **positive statement**.

The buyer has just put the earnest money down. "That is a highly regarded neighborhood. The grade school is one of the best in the city." As you hand the purchaser a **token**—a ballpoint pen with your agency's name on it—you say, "Here is the pen you signed with. It has my phone number on it if you have any further questions or if you want to tell me how much you like the place a few years from now."

In addition to reassurance, **point-of-purchase** selling is often called for. This is the case in many retail businesses. For example, the carpet cleaner tells you as you are receiving the ordered $49.95 special that for another $20 a special protective coating can be applied that will keep your carpet looking new.

Point-of-purchase selling can be helpful to the customer. (You have sold a piece of clothing for which the customer may not have the right color shoes. "Would you like some shoes to match this? Do you need a shirt in this color?") Point-of-purchase selling can also be annoying. Remember the long-term relationship that should be developed with the customer. If a possible need for the customer can be suggested, suggest it; if you are being pushy, forget it.

---

Q7-5 What can you do to reassure customers at point of purchase?

---

**Worksheet 21 Activities, Actions, Images Customers Like About
Your Product or Service (Refer to Worksheets 2, 10, 18)**

1.

2.

3.

4.

5.

6.

7.

8.

9.

10.

If an item is to be delivered it should be set up and functioning properly before the delivery person leaves. Play a tune on the piano. Make certain it is in tune and all the keys and pedals are operating. Leave a free music book as a thank-you.

If the computer is supposed to work, don't leave until the person who has purchased it knows how to do at least a few things on it. Make certain it is working. There are many dissatisfied microcomputer customers who will dump their current supplier as soon as there is competition. There are a lot of computer sales people who failed to deliver the total product (including buyer training) and who are no longer around.

Take a picture of the item with an instant developing camera. Have the owner in the picture too. This could be helpful to the buyer for insurance purposes as well as giving good feelings about the new purchase.

Make certain that the customer is satisfied at that point. Does the suit fit; are the shoes the right color; does the computer work properly?

Q7-6 What can you do to maximize customer satisfaction at the time of initial sale?

Delivery of the service or the production of it must be appropriate for the profession. One who pays $400 a day for a management seminar expects the presenter to be professionally attired.

The service should be delivered or produced in a **timely fashion.** A professional service deliverer who keeps customers waiting is giving the wrong message. The message is that the professional's time is more important than the client's. There are doctors, dentists, attorneys, opticians who make it a point to never keep their clients waiting. They may earn a dollar or two less a day by not scheduling so closely, but they always have a strong following regardless of the ups and downs of the economy.

Many service outfits will pick up loyal customers by letting their customers set an approximate hour rather than an approximate day or half-day when the delivery could be expected. The message is, "We know your time is important."

In our opinion, "the baker's dozen" is called for as a means of leaving the customer feeling good—satisfied with the deal. One remodeler "throws in" a want of the client that was not a part of the contracted items as a bonus—a "thank you for your business." When selling a pair of eyeglasses, offer a couple of free cases. When your income taxes are prepared offer a free "superduper form" on which to keep track of income and outgo for the next year to make tax figuring easier.

Q7-7 What could you utilize as a "baker's Dozen" idea?

The customer should feel good about taking possession of the good or service. It is completely appropriate to ask for **referrals**. It is also appropriate to ask for a **testimonial** if that could be used. Leave a brochure. Attach a tasteful sign on the fence saying "ABC Fence Co., Telephone #....." Leave a note pad for the phone with the company's name and address on it. Put on your thinking cap: there is a satisfied customer who would just as soon help you because you have just helped him or her.

Q7-8 What could you do at the initial point of sale to encourage referrals and repeat customers?

**Worksheet 22 Product and Service Delivery**

What will your response be to the customer when he or she places the order? (Q7-1, 6, Worksheet 21)

List the "baker's dozen" ideas you can think of that would be appropriate for your product or service. (Q7-7)

Are there point-of-purchase reminders that would be appropriate? (Q7-2, 7, 8)

Do you have a means of following up with a customer if his or her name is not already on a sales receipt? (Q7-8)

Did you ask for names of potential customers referred by the customer? (Q7-8)

## Customer Satisfaction Builds Success

Now that there are customers who are using the product or service, be concerned about whether or not they are able to use it. Are the **experiences positive?**

o  The computer sales outfit that calls the customer a few days after delivery is on the right track. Now is the time to see if the computer is still working fine. Is the customer able to get the programs working? Now is also the time to let the customer know of any changes or updates that might have occurred recently or any available training seminars.

> Q7-9 Describe any recent updates in your product or service that previous customers should know about.

o  The owner of the piano calls the renter after a month to make certain the piano is in tune. Maybe the owner even offers a couple of free lessons. That is a consumer conscious seller.

> Q7-10 What do you do that indicates you are customer-conscious?

o  A phone call to find out how it's going is worth it. This, in effect, is additional advertising to reassure the customer that it was a good purchase. Send a copy of the ad to the customer. Send additional information on related ideas or products or services.

> Q7-11 Would it be appropriate to call your customers to ask, "Is everything okay?"

o A week or two after purchase, mail a thank-you note. Attach a return stamped envelope with a **customer evaluation questionnaire.** How did the customer like the service? What could be improved? If it's appropriate to offer a coupon for a discount on some other item for such a valued customer, enclose one.

---

Q7-12 Are coupons a good promotion possibility for you?

---

o Some businesses are going to 24-hour-a-day, hot-line service. If you can't get the owner directly, get an answering service. Customer concerns should be noted. The television cable outfit that gets a call for service on Friday afternoon, but responds with, "I'm sorry, we cannot get a repair person to you until Monday" is begging for competition to shape it up.

---

Q7-13 Are your clients' concerns treated with respect?

---

o It may be appropriate to let customers know of other **related items** or sales they might be interested in. Is there an article on the future of computers that might be of interest? Send out copies. "Is there a better floppy disk than what came with the original sale? Come to find out those cheapies can gum up your machine. Here is a coupon good for one free blank disk or toward a $5 discount on a package of ten."

---

Q7-14 What items can you think of that are related to the original
       purchase item?

---

**Worksheet 23 Product Use and Service Experience**

Is your product or service being experienced favorably? (Q7-9, 11)

Is it worth finding out? (Q7-10)

What can you do to make certain that your customers are having a good experience with your products? (Q7-13)

Describe a way that will systematically help follow up on a customer within two weeks of delivery of purchase. (Q7-12)

What items can you suggest to complement the product or service recently purchased? (Q7-14)

## Customer Continuation, Cultivation, Satisfaction, Referral

The actual cost of securing a new customer is often high. Your best sources for developing new customers and increased sales come from current satisfied customers, and from enthusiastic employees. Numerous things can be done to help ensure that customers will buy again and that customers and employees tell others favorable things about the product or service.

o After a sales call, use a stamped self-addressed return card listing three different times and days from which the customer may choose to make an appointment.

o A reminder card can be sent regarding warranties (car dealers) or yearly appointments (doctors, dentists).

o A customer survey can be sent to those on your mailing list or researched in person, on site, to see how customers are doing and which additional products or services they might be interested in (marketing research questionnaire).

o Utilize a direct-mail campaign to distribute coupons good at local merchants and dealers (the appliance store sends out coupons for a free pint of berries from a local market to all customers who purchased an ice-cream maker last year).

o Give out free samples of your product (a blooming two-inch marigold to last year's garden center customers, broken cookie bits at the bakery cash register).

o Help support the local theater or symphony by purchasing groups of tickets at a discount and then passing that discount on to interested customers.

o Offer classes on your premises that may be of special interest to customers (a homebuilder class at the local lumber outlet, a CPR class to a local shopping center's clientele).

o Announce to your clientele an upcoming television special that deals with the particular service you provide.

o Have a special pre-sale for preferred customers before announcing it on local radio stations and newspapers (furniture store-moving or going-out-of-business sale).

Q7-15 How do you keep track of customers?  Leads?  Referrals?

Q7-16 Have you checked to see if your sales personnel enthusiastically
       support the product or service?

Q7-17 Are there other products or services that can be offered as part of
       the total package?

**Worksheet 24 Customer Satisfaction Builds Success**

Propose a plan to determine satisfaction after two weeks, six months, and one year. (Q7-15 to 17).

What additional products or services could you offer that customers might like? (Q7-17).

Describe some of the practices and procedures which you will do differently as a result of your thinking being jogged by ideas in this manual.

We've looked at marketing a product or service as a process that is customer focused. The marketing approach of "find a need and fill it" in a satisfactory manner is essential to achieve marketing success. We've presented ideas and worksheets from which you design a successful personalized marketing strategy. Now, please give us feedback through the publisher. What works? What do you want to see more of? What doesn't work? Did you find something that you'd like to tell others about?

If your marketing strategy works well locally, you may want to consider expanding to an international market. Refer to the next chapter on international marketing if you're interested.

In any case, keep in touch with changes in your target market characteristics, product or service differential advantages, the effectiveness of different advertising media, and many other factors which can affect your marketing success.

Good luck! May your enthusiasm, perseverence, and a sharp marketing strategy pay off!

# Chapter 8
# International Marketing

International marketing requires a different approach than domestic marketing. The small firm owner or manager can use marketing research to help decide if international activity is a viable business alternative.

There are numerous reasons for expanding overseas, probably including some you don't know about. If you can answer "yes" to any of the questions in Worksheet 25, you may want to consider expanding to international markets.

## Selecting a Target Market, Product, Country

One of the major deterrents to owners and managers of small firms interested in entering foreign trade markets has been the lack of a simple procedure to obtain needed information, contact points, organizational facilities, promotional activities, documentation, and answers to numerous questions.

The International Trade Administration of the United States Department of Commerce has in the developmental stage a program known by its acronym, **WITS (Worldwide Information and Trade System)**. This program utilizes a computer which is linked with terminals across the United States and around the world for collecting and disseminating foreign trade information.

When this program becomes fully operative, export information in the form of abstracts from publications of public and private agencies and organizations around the world will become readily available. Also included among the services offered by WITS will be sales leads to thousands of potential business contacts in the United States and foreign countries; actual offers to export or import specific products; current statistics on market conditions by products and markets; schedule of promotional events; and helpful guidance on how to get started in exporting—the basic steps and procedures—and where to get help. Its vast data resources will provide fast, convenient access to more up-to-date marketing intelligence than any other single information system available.

Currently, much of this export information is available for nine foreign countries: United Kingdom, France, Japan, Hong Kong, Singapore, Mexico, Brazil, Saudi Arabia, and Nigeria. For only a nominal fee, WITS information on these countries may be obtained from the U.S. Department of Commerce district offices in five cities: Boston, Chicago, Seattle, Los Angeles, and Dallas—or by contacting the WITS staff in Washington, D.C.

Q8-1 What worldwide information would be useful to you? Which countries and product markets are you interested in?

Additionally, several other agencies of the federal government can now furnish information on exporting, importing, economic and marketing information, financing opportunities and documentation requirements, customs, regulations, transportation facilities, and other related topics. Among these agencies are the **Overseas Private Investment Corporation (OPIC)**, the **Agency for International Development (AID)**, and the **Small Business Administration (SBA)**. In addition, the **United Nations** and the **World Bank** send missions and study teams to prepare reports on economic, political, and social conditions in most trading nations of the world.

A prospective exporter may be able to obtain SBA help in securing funds to expand production facilities to meet foreign demand, finance basic overseas market development costs, and to purchase materials and labor required to perform an export sales contract. Assistance is available primarily through the Small Business Administration guarantee loan program. However, SBA financial support cannot be used to establish or expand a business located outside of the United States. This type of support may be available through programs of other U.S. government agencies.

The **Export-Import Bank** maintains a special office to provide information and services, discount loans, and foreign bank credits to small exporters. It also sponsors several financing programs. Under the Export Credit Insurance Program, an exporter can apply for export credit, commercial, and political risk insurance. Applications are made through a national insurance broker of a Foreign Credit Insurance Association regional office. The Commercial Bank Exporter Guarantee Program covers direct sales of U.S.-origin capital and quasi-capital goods to qualified buyers. Coverage ranges from 181 days to five years. The program is operated by 300 U.S. commercial banks. The Co-operative Financing Facility Program helps make credit available to small and medium-size foreign buyers through financing by local foreign banks in their own countries.

**Worksheet 25 Exporting and Licensing Considerations**
(Check the considerations that apply for your business.)

___ Is your domestic market stagnant? (If you manufacture regular file drawers and do not plan to change, the United States' move to computers may decrease the need for traditional file cabinets—possibly a developing country would be a market for traditional file cabinets).

___ Is the level of economic activity in the industry decreasing? (The big shake-out in computer software and computer game firms may indicate too much supply for current demand. Maybe games were a passing fad. Or have Teddy Bears run their course?) It may be necessary to look increasingly to the international arena for fulfilling your marketing sales goal.

___ Do you have excess productive capacity? (A computer being used 26% of the time, machines not utilized for several hours, or employees on involuntary part-time or short workweek schedules may indicate that you could produce more if new markets were found or license others to utilize your excess capacity.

___ Are there some possible tax advantages from importing certain materials and components that could be used in products to be exported? (There is a possibility of a refund of customs duty for some materials. There are also free trade zones in operation in 75 countries, situated outside customs' territory. If goods are imported for processing, assembly and re-exporting, you may not have to pay duties or federal excise tax.)

___ Are you a small manufacturer of products made from domestic materials who might be able to get significant tax breaks by exporting products under criteria established by the Domestic International Sales Corporations (DISCS)?

___ Are you quite sure that there are other countries, or at least one specific one, in which your product or service could be sold with little or no modifications? (You manufacture a thermos that will hold heat for 48 hours due to a miniature solar operated heating unit which adds approximately one-half inch in length to the thermos. There should be other countries that could use this thermos.)

___ Are you aware from your travels or information from other sources of certain products or services that might be appropriate for a foreign market? (You are now Oasis Press producing a line of self-help books for people in business or wanting to go into business. Last time you went to London you noticed that there were a total of two books in Harrod's on "going into business." One might want to research the need for such books and see if overseas sources could be secured to do such production.

___ Do you have one or several good contacts in other countries who might make good distributors or manufacturers? (Having a trusted person who knows the cultural ins and outs, legalities, and politics of doing business in another country is critical. Building up a sales system or production system from scratch can be a long, arduous process even if you know the language, the customs, the politics, and the markets. The networks need to be built. If you have access to those resources, it might signal a possible opportunity.)

___ Are there certain processes in the manufacture or assembly of your product that could be accomplished more cheaply or with higher quality elsewhere? (Buying cloth to have it made into clothing in Hong Kong then shipping back to the United States may be cheaper than manufacturing here.)

A company interested in establishing facilities in developing countries should be aware of the Overseas Private Investment Corporation Program (OPIC). As an agency of the U.S. government, OPIC will, on a selective basis, enter into cost-sharing arrangements with a U.S. firm to study the feasibility of an opportunity the firm has identified. It provides project financing in countries where conventional financing institutions are reluctant or unable to lend. It also provides three types of insurance protection to cover the risk of currency inconvertability, expropriation, and loss or damage caused by war, revolution, or insurrection.

OPIC provides several specific services to smaller U.S. companies. They include a reduced insurance registration fee, OPIC payments for services of licensed insurance brokers to smaller companies obtaining OPIC insurance, grants for certain project reconnaissance travel, expanded funding of up to 75% of agreed costs of feasibility studies, assumption by OPIC of certain legal or consultants' fees incurred in establishing or operating a project, and assistance in setting up financial controls.

The SBA provides aid to potential small business or minority exporters through two programs. The Management Assistance Program can include:

o One-on-one counseling by students or volunteers with international trade experience.

o Business management training.

o Assistance from professional consulting firms.

o Provision of management and marketing publications.

Export workshops and training programs are cosponsored by SBA District Offices with the Commerce Department and others interested in international trade. The Financial Assistance Program makes available funds that can be used to purchase equipment or materials necessary for the manufacture and sale of products overseas or for working capital. They may not be used to establish a joint venture abroad. For eligible borrowers, SBA will guarantee up to 90% of a private lending institution's loan.

Other organizations that may be able to help are:

o International Chain of Industrial and Technical Advertising Agencies, 2700 U.S. Highway 22, Union, New Jersey 07083.

o Magazine Publishers Association, International Committee, 575 Lexington Avenue, New York, New York 10002. Publishes list of magazines with overseas circulation.

o Packaging Institute U.S.A., 342 Madison Avenue, New York, New York 10017. An excellent source of information on export packaging.

U.S. Publications magazines published for circulation abroad can be invaluable:

o  *The American Exporter,* Johnson International Publications, New York.

o  *Modern Government/National Development,* International Publications, Westport, Connecticut.

o  *World Project,* International Publications, Westport, Connecticut.

Market potential and growth as well as risk associated with entry can be evaluated through published resources. **Business International,** for example, publishes information on three indices for countries in Western and Eastern Europe, the Middle East, Latin America, Asia, Africa, and Australia: market growth, market intensity, and market size. The specific variables included in each of these indices vary somewhat from region to region, reflecting different market characteristics.

Additional useful publications include annual surveys of the Middle East, Africa, Asia, the Pacific, and Latin America and the Caribbean, published by the World of Information. The *Price Waterhouse Country Information* guides and Dun and Bradstreet's *Exporters Encyclopedia* also provide much useful information on foreign investment opportunities, exchange controls and investment incentives.

Some published sources relating to specific product markets are available. The U.S. Department of Commerce publishes detailed global market surveys covering 20 to 30 of the best foreign markets for a given industry, such as graphics, industrial or medical equipment, and computers. The advantage of these reports is that they provide an easily accessible, predigested survey of world markets. Attractive market prospects can thus be selected by matching a specific product range with a company's competitive advantage in supplying that market. The surveys are, however, only available for the limited number of industries identified by the Department of Commerce as prime prospects for the development of export potential.

## Insurance

The Foreign Credit Insurance Association (FCIA) administers the export credit insurance program on behalf of member insurance companies. The Export-Import Bank of the United States covers commercial credit risks (mainly foreign insolvency or prolonged payment default by an overseas buyer) as well as political risks, including such hazards as war, confiscation, and expropriation. FCIA and the Export-Import Bank offer a short-term insurance policy specifically designed to meet the requirements of small business exporters. The policy is available to firms with a net worth of $2 million or less and average annual export sales during the preceding two years of $350,000 or less, and which have not previously used FCIA or Export-Import Bank programs. The special coverage is provided for a two-year period. The policy covers 100% of the political risk and 95% of the commercial loss risk involved in the financial portion of the transaction. It frees the smaller exporter from the "first loss" risk provisions which are found in regular policies.

Q8-2 Which of the above agencies, and what other agencies, would have helpful information?

## Other Things to Know

Besides general information on exports of various products, it is necessary to have a basic knowledge of the country in which the company plans to operate. P. R. Harris and R. T . Moran, in their book, *Managing Cultural Differences,* recommend familiarity with the following:

o Who are the important people, both current and past, in politics, sports, and the arts?

o Politics, especially current political leaders and their titles, the major political parties, the name of the parliament or legislature.

o Geography: the name and approximate populations of major cities and bordering counties.

o Business and social customs: the courtesies that should be observed. How do people greet each other? How do they say goodbye? Is gift giving a custom? What is the normal working day? What are some dominant business values? Should you be on time or late for a meeting? Who pays for business lunches?

o Social structure and attitudes: What are important class and ethnic divisions? Is consensus valued more than individuality? Are Americans liked or disliked, and for what reasons? What is your attitude toward the society?

Q8-3 What are the cultural differences involved in your overseas target market?

## Choosing the Distribution Channel

Once the decision to enter the international markets has been made, the firm must choose an appropriate distribution channel. Two options, exporting and licensing, will be mentioned here. Exporting appears to be the most attractive, least complicated, and most utilized option for small firms entering international markets.

Export distribution alternatives may be divided into general classes, direct and indirect export. **Direct exporting** utilizes a go-between or final user located in the foreign market. The selling firm usually retains the responsibility for transporting the product. And conversely, **indirect exporting** utilizes a go-between located in the U.S. who usually assumes responsibility for transporting the goods overseas. Firms with limited experience generally prefer the indirect route with a local link. A number of indirect exporting options are available; three of the more common forms are the use of selling groups, export management companies, and export trading companies.

**Selling groups** are consortiums of various firms that cooperate to sell their merchandise abroad. In this case, companies are permitted to associate to carry out foreign trade, and are exempted from antitrust action by the Webb-Pomerene Export Trade Act of 1981. Large and small firms can take many advantages of selling groups. For example, a larger firm may agree to market, through its established channels of distribution, the products of a smaller firm. The condition is known as complementary marketing or "piggy-backing." It provides ready distribution outlets to the small firm and allows the large firm to balance or complete its product line.

**Export management companies (EMCs)** typically identify markets, contact customers, negotiate sales, and handle the necessary paperwork and credit arrangements for the selling firm. A number of firms selling non-competing products for a commission are represented by the EMC. The use of an EMC may be particularly advantageous for small firms with limited international volume, since a minimum investment in capital and personnel is required. The Commerce Department lists over 1100 EMCs in the United States in its *U.S. Export Management Companies Directory*.

Export trading companies are the product of the Export Trading Company (ETC) Act of 1982, passed to help counteract the growing U.S. trade deficits since 1970. This legislation is intended to facilitate export development by all U.S. firms through the formation of export trading companies, through modifications, in the application of antitrust legislation, through reduction in export financing restrictions, and through the involvement of banks and financial institutions as investors in export trading companies.

Banks appear to be one of the primary vehicles for the successful formation of ETCs. Small to medium-sized banks themselves can look to ETCs as a means of getting into international marketing and banking services. The new act enables banks to sponsor or manage a consortium of local businesses in the form of an ETC in order to compete internationally.

**Worksheet 26 Export Target Markets**

List the sources of information that would be helpful for background on exporting. (Q8-1 to 3)

What basic questions about the target market country do you need to know? (Q8-2, 3, Worksheet 5)

This act is seen as a tremendous boon for small and medium-sized firms, since the trading companies can provide marketing, transportation, financial, and other related services.

While the exact effect and influence of ETCs on the export activities of small firms is yet to be determined, they appear to be a particularly attractive option for small firms entering exporting. Information on export trading companies and necessary guidelines are available from the Department of Commerce.

In contrast to indirect methods, **direct exporting** enables a firm to deal directly with foreign customers through sales people or distributors.

o **Sales representatives** serve as agents for the small business and may call directly on foreign retailers. They are paid a commission and have no responsibility for the merchandise.

o **Foreign distributors** purchase from U.S. companies and resell to other foreign firms. Sell Overseas America has two publications, *Showcase USA* and *Yankee Trader,* which list names of foreign buyers and what products, they are looking for.

Time, energy, and money must be spent visiting the country and talking to the ultimate users of one's product to learn firsthand which distributors are preferred, and why. Such efforts may be beyond the means of many small firms. But the Department of Commerce may be particularly useful. It maintains lists of distributors by field of activity and country.

Although the economic environment in the United States favors exporting, some export restrictions exist. Foremost is the requirement for an export license. Two types of export license are available, general licenses and validated licenses. A general license permits exporting without an export document. A validated license is a more formal application and is required for exporting "strategic" goods or exporting to "unfriendly" countries. It is the duty of the Department of Commerce to determine precisely which type of license will be required of a firm.

The distinction between direct and indirect exporting is important. The implications of choosing one or the other are significant. For example, in a direct method, the seller must learn about the business, marketing, and cultural conditions of the foreign country. Details such as special packaging, exchange fluctuations, collection problems, and shipping charges must be attended to. However, in an indirect method, such details are usually not as much the seller's concern.

Q8-4 List the advantages to you of indirect and direct selling methods:

   o Indirect: (Selling groups, Export Management Companies, and
      Export Trading Companies)

   o Direct: (Sales representatives and foreign distributors)

## Foreign Licensing

Basically, foreign licensing covers all sorts of contractual arrangements whereby the small business (licensor) provides its patents, trademarks, manufacturing expertise, or technical services to a foreign business (licensee). In return, the licensee pays a royalty on the sale of the product. Typically, the small business owner does not become involved with the daily operation of the details of production and distribution. The licensee tends to run the operations of its business, and acquires additional know-how or an opportunity to legally sell a product, service, or process that is owned by the licensor.

Donald Weimauch and Arthur Larglor list the advantages and disadvantages of licensing in the October 1983 issue of *Journal of Small Business Management:*

**Advantages**

o Minimum capital outlay.

o A more realistic means of international expansion for the high-tech firm than exporting.

o Ease of access to foreign markets, especially compared to equity investment.

o Savings in tariff and transportation costs.

o Foreign government approval, because licensing brings technology into the country with fewer strings and costs.

o Potential for the licensees to become partners and contributors in improving the learning curve or technology.

o Support for production, marketing, and post-sale servicing.

**Disadvantages**

o Having the licensee become a competitor after the contract expires.

o Experiencing limited returns (usually three to five percent of sales as compared to more for exporting or equity investment).

o Getting the licensee to meet contractual expectations.

o Managing the relationship as conditions and circumstances evolve.

o Overcoming conflicts or misunderstandings about production or marketing.

o Adjusting the licensor's products or services to fit the markets of the licensee.

o Maintaining the integrity and independence of both the licensor and licensee.

The drawbacks can be significant. Many small firms are often afraid of becoming involved in complex contractual negotiations when it seems easier to export. And many businesses will consider exporting or even international equity investment before exploring potentially profitable ventures through licensing. Also, many managers, especially in small business, are disturbed by the thought of sharing technology and trade secrets with a foreign business. Consequently, international licensing is not pursued by most smaller firms, which thus miss out on profitable opportunities.

---

Q8-5 What are the advantages and disadvantages of using foreign licensing arrangements for your business?

---

## Worksheet 27 Approaches to International Marketing

Summarize the advantages and disadvantages of various approaches to international marketing (Q8-1 to 5, Worksheets 25, 26)

|  | Advantages | Disadvantages |
|---|---|---|
| Indirect exporting |  |  |
| Direct exporting |  |  |
| Licensing |  |  |
| Tax aspects |  |  |

What do you plan to do now?

# Appendix A Pricing for Retailers

A retailer's prices influence the quantities of various items that consumers will buy, which in turn affect total revenue and profit. Hence, correct pricing decisions are a key to successful retail management. With this in mind, the following checklist of 52 questions has been developed to assist small retailers in making systematic, informed decisions regarding pricing strategies and tactics.

This checklist should be especially useful to a new retailer who is making pricing decisions for the first time. However, established retailers, including successful ones, can also benefit from this. They may use it as a reminder of all the individual pricing decisions they should review periodically. And it may also be used in training new employees who will have pricing authority.

## The Central Concept of Markup

A major step toward making a profit in retailing is selling merchandise for more than it costs you. This difference between cost of merchandise and retail price is called **markup** (or occasionally **markdown**). From an arithmetic standpoint, markup is calculated as follows:

Dollar Markup = Retail Price - Cost of the Merchandise

$$\text{Percentage Markup (as a percent of Sales Price)} = \frac{\text{Dollar Markup}}{\text{Retail Price}}$$

or

$$\text{Percentage Markup (as a percent of Cost)} = \frac{\text{Dollar Markup}}{\text{Cost Price}}$$

If an item costs $6.50 and you feel consumers will buy it at $10.00, the dollar markup is $3.50 (which is $10.00 - $6.50). Going one step further, the markup as a percent of sales price is 35 percent (which is $3.50 ÷ $10.00). Anyone involved in retail pricing should be as knowledgeable about these two formulas as about the name and preferences of his or her best customer!

---

This pricing worksheet has been adapted from SBA Aid #158: "A Pricing Checklist for Small Retailers" by Bruce J. Walker, Associate Professor of Marketing at Arizona State University, Tempe, Arizona (first printed in June 1976).'

Two other key points about markup should be mentioned. First, the cost of **merchandise** used in calculating markup consists of the base invoice price for the merchandise **plus** any transportation charges minus any quantity and cash discounts given by the seller. Second, **retail price**, rather than cost, is ordinarily used in calculating percentage markup. The reason for this is that when other operating figures such as wages, advertising expenses, and profits are expressed as a percentage, all are based on retail price rather than cost of the merchandise being sold.

## Target Consumers and the Retailing Mix

In this section, your attention is directed to price as it relates to your potential customers. These questions examine your merchandise, location, promotion, and customer services that will be combined with price in attempting to satisfy shoppers and make a profit. After some questions, brief commentary is provided.

1. **Is the relative price of this item very important to your target consumers?**

   The importance of price depends on the specific product and on the specific individual. Some shoppers are very price-conscious, others want convenience and knowledgeable sales personnel. Because of these variations, you need to learn about your customers' desires in relation to different products. Having sales personnel seek feedback from shoppers is a good starting point.

2. **Are prices based on estimates of the number of units that consumers will demand at various price levels?**

   Demand-oriented pricing such as this is superior to cost-oriented pricing. In the cost approach, a predetermined amount is added to the cost of the merchandise, whereas in the demand approach, price considerations depnd on what consumers are willing to pay.

3. **Have you established a price range for the product?**

   The cost of merchandise will be at one end of the price range and the level above which consumers will not buy the product at the other end.

4. **Have you considered what price strategies would be compatible with your store's total retailing mix that includes merchandise, location, promotion, and services?**

5. **Will trade-ins be acceptable as part of the purchase price on items such as appliances and television sets?**

## Supplier and Competitor Considerations

This set of questions looks outside your firm to two factors that you cannot directly control—suppliers and competitors.

6. **Do you have a final pricing authority?**

   With the repeal of fair trade laws, "yes" answers will be more common than in previous years. Still, a supplier can control retail prices by refusing to deal with non-conforming stores (a tactic which may be illegal) or by selling to you on consignment.

7. **Do you know how your direct competitors' prices are set?**

8. **Do you regularly review competitor's ads to obtain information on their prices?**

9. **Is your store large enough to employ either a full-time or part-time comparison shopper?**

   These last three questions emphasize the point that you must watch competitors' prices so that your prices will not be far out of line—too high or too low—without good reason. Of course, there may be a good reason for out-of-the-ordinary prices, such as seeking a special price image.

## A Price Level Strategy

Selecting a general level of prices in relation to competition is a key strategic decision, perhaps the most important.

10. **Should your overall strategy be to sell at prevailing market price levels?**

    The other alternatives are an above-the-market strategy or a below-the-market strategy.

11. **Should competitors' temporary price reductions ever be matched?**

12. **Could private-brand merchandise be obtained in order to avoid direct price competition?**

## Calculating Planned Initial Markup

In this section you will have to look inside your business, taking into account sales, expenses, and profits before setting prices. The point is that your initial markup must be large enough to cover anticipated expenses and reductions and still produce a satisfactory profit.

13. **Have you estimated sales, operating expenses, and reductions for the next selling season?**

14. **Have you established a profit objective for the next selling season?**

15. **Given estimated sales, expenses, and reductions, have you planned initial markup?**

    The figure is calculated with the following formula:

    $$\text{Initial markup percentage} = \frac{\text{Operating expenses} + \text{Reductions} + \text{Profits}}{\text{Net sales} + \text{Reductions}}$$

    Reductions consist of markdowns, stock shortages, and employee and customer discounts. The following example uses dollar amounts, but the estimates can also be percentages. If a retailer anticipates $94,000 in sales for a particular department, $34,000 in expenses, and $6,000 in reductions, and if the retailer desires a $4,000 profit, initial markup percentage can be calculated:

    $$\text{Initial markup percentage} = \frac{\$34,000 + \$6,000 + \$4,000}{\$94,000 + \$6,000}$$
    $$= 44\%$$

    The resulting figure, 44% in this example, indicates what size initial markup is needed on the average in order to make the desired profits.

16. **Could it be appropriate to have different initial markup figures for various lines of merchandise or services?**

    You would seriously consider this when some lines have much different characteristics than others. For instance, a clothing retailer might logically have different initial markup figures for suits, shirts and pants, and accessories. (Various merchandise characteristics are covered in an upcoming section.) You may want those items with the highest turnover rates to carry the lowest initial markup.

## Store Policies

Having calculated an initial markup figure, you could proceed to set prices on your merchandise. But an important decision such as this should not be rushed. Instead, you should consider additional factors which suggest what would be the best price.

17. **Is your tentative price compatible with established store policies?**

    Policies are guidelines indicating appropriate methods or actions in different situations. If established with care, they can save you time in decision making and provide for consistent treatment of shoppers. Specific policy areas that you should consider are as follows:

18. **Will a one-price system, under which the same price is charged every purchaser of a particular item, be used on all items?**

    The alternative is to negotiate price with consumers.

19. **Will odd-ending prices, such as $1.98 and $44.95, be more appealing to your customers than even-ending prices?**

20. **Will consumers buy more if multiple pricing, such as 2 for $8.50, is used?**

21. **Should any "loss leader" offerings (selected products with quite low, less profitable prices) be used?**

22. **Have the characteristics of an effective leader offering been considered?**

    Ordinarily, a leader offering needs the following char- acteristics to accomplish its purpose of generating much shopper traffic: used by most people, bought frequently, very familiar regular price, and not a large expenditure for consumers.

23. **Would price lining, the practice of setting up distinct price points (such as $5.00, $7.50, and $10.00) and then marking all related merchandise at these points, be used?**

24. **Would price lining by means of zones (such as $5.00-$7.50 and $12.50-$15.00) be more appropriate than price points?**

25. **Will cents-off coupons be used in newspaper ads or mailed to selected consumers on any occasion?**

26. **Would periodic special sales, combining reduced prices and heavier advertising, be consistent with the business image you are seeking?**

27. **Do certain items have greater appeal than others when they are part of a special sale?**

28. **Has the impact of various sale items or profits been considered?**

    Sale prices may mean little or no profit on these items. Still, the special sale may contribute to total profits by bringing in shoppers who may also buy some regular-price (and profitable) merchandise, and by attracting new customers. Also, you should avoid featuring items that require a large amount of labor, which in turn would reduce or erase profits. For instance, according to this criterion, shirts would be a better special sale item than men's suits that often require free alterations.

29. **Will "rain checks" be issued to customers who come in for special-sale merchandise that is temporarily out of stock?**

    You should give particular attention to this decision since rain checks are required in some situations. Consult your lawyer or the regional Federal Trade Commission office for specific advice.

## Nature of the Merchandise

In this section you will be considering how selected characteristics of particular merchandise affect planned initial markup.

30. **Did you get a "good deal" on the wholesale price of this merchandise?**

31. **Is this item at the peak of its popularity?**

32. **Are handling and selling costs relatively high due to the product being bulky, having a low turnover rate, or requiring much personal selling, installation, or alterations?**

33. **Are relatively large levels of reductions expected due to markdowns, spoilage, breakage, or theft?**

    With respect to the preceding four questions, "yes" answers suggest the possibility of or need for larger-than-normal initial markups. For example, very fashionable clothing often will carry a higher markup than basic clothing such as underwear because the particular fashion may suddenly lose its appeal to consumers (shorter product life cycle).

34. **Will customer services such as delivery, alterations, gift wrapping, and installation be free of charge to customers? The alternative is to charge for some or all of these services.**

## Environmental Considerations

The questions in this section focus your attention on three factors outside your business, namely economic conditions, laws, and consumerism.

35. **If your state has an unfair sales practices act that requires minimum markups on certain merchandise, do your prices comply with this statute?**

36. **Are economic conditions in your trading area abnormal?**

    Consumers tend to be more price-conscious when the economy is depressed, suggesting that lower-than-normal markups may be needed to be competitive. On the other hand, shoppers are less price-conscious when the economy is booming, which would permit larger markups on a selective basis.

37. **Are the ways in which prices are displayed and promoted compatible with the consumerist call for more straightforward price information?**

38. **Is it feasible to use unit pricing, in which an item's cost per some standard measure is indicated?**

Having asked (and hopefully answered) more than three dozen questions, you are indeed ready to establish retail prices. When you have decided on an appropriate percentage markup, 35% on a garden hose for example, the next step is to determine what percentage of the still unknown retail price is represented by the cost figure. The basic markup formula is simply rearranged to do this:

Cost = Retail price - Markup

Cost = 100% - 35% = 65%

Then the dollar cost, say $3.25 for the garden hose, is plugged into the following formula to arrive at the retail price:

$$\text{Retail price} = \frac{\text{Dollar cost}}{\text{Percentage cost}} = \frac{\$3.25}{65\%} = \$5.00$$

One other consideration is necessary:

39. **Is the retail price consistent with your planned initial markups?**

## Adjustments

It would be ideal if all items actually sold at their original retail prices. But we know that things are not always ideal. Therefore, a section on price adjustments is necessary.

40. **Are additional markups called for, because wholesale prices have increased or because an item's low price causes consumers to question its quality?**

41. **Should employees be given purchase discounts?**

42. **Should any groups of customers, such as students or senior citizens, be given purchase discounts?**

43. **When markdowns appear necessary, have you first considered other alternatives such as retaining price but changing another element of the retailing mix or storing the merchandise until the next selling season?**

44. **Has an attempt been made to identify causes of markdowns so that steps can be taken to minimize the number of avoidable buying, selling, and pricing errors that cause markdowns?**

45. **Has the relationship between timing and size of markdowns been taken into account?**

   In general, markdown taken early in the selling season or shortly after sales slow down can be smaller than late markdowns. Whether an early or late markdown would be more appropriate in a particular situation depends on several things: your assessment of how many consumers might still be interested in the product, the size of the initial markup, and the amount remaining in stock.

46. **Would a schedule of automatic markdowns after merchandise has been in stock for specified intervals be appropriate?**

47. **Is the size of the markdown "just enough" to stimulate purchases?**

Of course, this question is difficult—perhaps impossible—to answer. Nevertheless, it stresses the point that you have to carefully observe the effects of different size markdowns so that you can eventually acquire some insights into what size markdowns are "just enough" for different kinds of merchandise.

48. **Has a procedure been worked out for markdowns on price-lined merchandise?**

49. **Is the markdown price calculated from the off-retail percentage?**

This question gets you into the arithmetic of markdowns. Usually, you first tentatively decide on the percentage amount price must be marked down to excite customers. For example, if you think a 25% markdown will be necessary to sell a lavender sofa, the dollar amount of the markdown is calculated as follows:

Dollar markdown = Off-retail percentage x Previous retail price

Dollar markdown = 25% x $500 = $125

Then the markdown price is obtained by subtracting the dollar markdown from the previous retail price. Hence, the sofa would be $375.00 after taking the markdown.

50. **Has cost of the merchandise been considered before setting the markdown price?**

This is not to say that a markdown price should never be lower than cost; on the contrary, a price that low may be your only hope of generating any revenue from the item. But cost should be considered to make sure that below-cost markdown prices are the exception in your outlet rather than being so common that your total profits are really hurt.

51. **Have procedures for recording the dollar amounts, percentages, and probable causes of markdowns been set up?**

Analyzing markdowns is very important since it can provide information that will assist in calculating planned initial markup, in decreasing errors that cause markdowns, and in evaluating suppliers.

You may be weary from thinking your way through the preceding sections, but don't overlook an important final question:

52. **Have you marked the calendar for a periodic review of your pricing decisions?**

Rather than "laying an egg" due to careless pricing decisions, this checklist should help you lay a solid foundation of effective prices as you try to build retail profits.

# Appendix B
# Sample Questionnaire & Letter

Bristol, Bagley, Brown and Horner
8th and Liverpool Avenue
Chicago, Illinois

Dear Subscriber,

Will you help make *Chicago Woman* the best magazine it can be?

We are an independent research group conducting a survey of *Chicago Woman's* readership. The purpose of this research is to obtain important information on how you feel about your magazine. Your answers will help *Chicago Woman* to decide what direction the magazine will take in the future.

Please take a few moments to complete the enclosed questionnaire, and return it in the stamped reply envelope. Your response by February 25th is essential for the success of this survey.

All answers will be strictly confidential. Thank you for your participation. We look forward to your response.

Sincerely,

Helena Bagley
BBBH Research Group

1. Please tell us why you chose to subscribe to *Chicago Woman* magazine

   __ for personal use     __ for office use by clients
   __ gift subscription     __ other (please specify) _____

2. How many people do you share your copy of *Chicago Woman* magazine with?

   _none   _one  _two  _three  _four  _more than four

3. How often do you read the following columns? (please circle a number)

|  | never |  |  |  | every issue |
|---|---|---|---|---|---|
| Sound Mind and Body (health) | 1 | 2 | 3 | 4 | 5 |
| Managing Up, Down and Sideways (business) | 1 | 2 | 3 | 4 | 5 |
| Consumer Savvy (consumer issues) | 1 | 2 | 3 | 4 | 5 |
| The Last Laugh (humor) | 1 | 2 | 3 | 4 | 5 |
| Spree! (local shopping) | 1 | 2 | 3 | 4 | 5 |

4. On a scale of one to five, how well has *Chicago Woman* met your expectations as a local woman's magazine? (please circle a number)

   has not met
   my expectations    1     2     3     4     5    has totally met
   my expectations

5. On a scale of one to five, how interested are you in seeing more articles on the following subjects? (please circle a number)

|  | not interested |  |  |  | very interested |
|---|---|---|---|---|---|
| Professional/career | 1 | 2 | 3 | 4 | 5 |
| Investment/money | 1 | 2 | 3 | 4 | 5 |
| Local personalities | 1 | 2 | 3 | 4 | 5 |
| Health care | 1 | 2 | 3 | 4 | 5 |
| Marriage/relationships | 1 | 2 | 3 | 4 | 5 |
| Arts/entertainment | 1 | 2 | 3 | 4 | 5 |
| Home/interior design | 1 | 2 | 3 | 4 | 5 |
| Food preparation | 1 | 2 | 3 | 4 | 5 |
| Fashion/appearance | 1 | 2 | 3 | 4 | 5 |
| Travel/recreation | 1 | 2 | 3 | 4 | 5 |
| Restaurant reviews | 1 | 2 | 3 | 4 | 5 |
| Political issues | 1 | 2 | 3 | 4 | 5 |
| Sports | 1 | 2 | 3 | 4 | 5 |
| Family/children | 1 | 2 | 3 | 4 | 5 |
| Culture/education | 1 | 2 | 3 | 4 | 5 |

6. Please check the local publications that you consistently read:

__Chicago Tribune __Chicago Examiner __The Weekly Shopper
__Argus __Journal American __Arts Line __Midwest News
__other (specify) _____ __None

7. Please check the radio stations that you consistently listen to:

__KIRO __KOMO __KING-AM __KING-FM __KUBE __KMPS __KZOK
__KVI __KJR __KBRD __KSEA __KISW __KJET __KYYK
__KSPL __KSLY __KEZX __KIXI
__other (Specify)_____

8. How do you spend your leisure time? (please check as many as appropriate)

Entertainment                                              Hobbies

__movies          __gardening          __needlework/knitting
__theatre         __photography        __home improvement projects
__symphony        __painting           __other (please specify)
__ballet          __antiques
__opera           __collecting         _____
__art galleries   __music              _____
__professional    __writing            _____
   sporting events __reading            _____

Recreation Activities

__golf                __SCUBA diving
__horseback riding    __bowling
__tennis              __aerobics/fitness
__racquetball         __fishing/hunting
__boating             __mountain climbing
__skiing              __hiking
__water skiing        __softball
__jogging             __soccer
__other (specify) _____

9. To which of the following types of organizations do you belong?

Social                    Community                        Business

__country club    __chamber of commerce    __trade organization
__yacht club      __school board/PTA       __professional group
__alumni club     __hospital board         __other (specify)
__fraternal club  __political organization
__other (specify) __church or religious     _____
                  __other (specify)
_____                              _____
                  _____
_____     _____            _____

A - 11

10. Age: __under 18 __18-25 __26-35 __36-45 __46-55 __56-65 __over 65

11. Sex: __female __male

12. Marital status: __single __married __separated __divorced __widowed

13. How many children do you have in the following age groups?
    (please indicate number)

    __under 5 __6-10 years __11-18 years __over 18 years __no children

14. What is your total household income?

    __under $15,000       __$15,000-24,999       __$25,000-34,999
    __$35,000-44,999      __$45,000-54,999       __$55,000-64,999
    __over $65,000

15. Please indicate the highest level of education you have completed:

    __high school or less  __some college
    __college graduate     __post graduate

16. Please indicate, by letter, your occupation and, if applicable, your spouse's occupation

    _____ self  _____spouse

    A. secretarial/clerical    G. entrepreneur     M. teacher/professor
    B. food services           H. attorney         N. retail/wholesale
    C. government worker       I. manager          O. engineer
    D. physician/dentist       J. paralegal        P. retired
    E. other health care       K. laborer          Q. unemployed
    F. banking/financial       L. homemaker        R. other (specify)
       service                                        self_____
                                                      spouse_____

Please return the completed questionnaire in the envelope provided. Thank you.

# Appendix C
# Marketing Basics Revisited:
# Keys to Success in the Software Business

Lewis Conner[1]

Ken Germann

Overattention to technical sophistication and media hoopla can mask the importance of mastering the basic components of a successful marketing strategy:
product, place, promotion and price. The application software industry provides
the latest opportunity to relearn this fundamental truth.

## Introduction

The applications software market is booming. Users can live with one microcomputer; their appetite for software to solve technical problems or provide
specific business-related capabilities is insatiable. More importantly, there is room
for the little guy to successfully compete with industry giants like IBM, MicroPro
and VisiCorp. How big is the market? How can a small firm selling business or
technical software make it in this industry? What are the critical factors for
success? This article, based on a study of industry data and interviews with software entrepreneurs, attempts to answer these questions.[2] In addition it will
become evident that attention to marketing fundamentals is the key to
developing a successful business strategy. The need for sound marketing is often
hidden in the initial acceptance of new fashionable products. But these very
basics are essential to long term survival.

---

[1]Lewis "Red" Conner is Assistant Professor of Management at San
Francisco State University. Ken Germann is an attorney in Oakland,
California. "Marketing Basics Revisited: Keys to Success in the Software
Business" is reprinted with permission. It was originally published in *The
San Francisco State University School of Business Journal,* Winter, 1984.'

[2]Nine S.F. Bay Area software firms participated in our survey. In-depth,
structured interviews were conducted with their marketing executives to
ascertain the firms' business goals and major marketing strategies.

## The Market

The market for microcomputer software is new, less than a decade old. Yet sales of programs performing business and technical functions were estimated at over $230 million in 1982. This same source projects business and technical software sales to increase more than fivefold by 1987, to more than $1.56 billion.[3] (Other market segments, such as education, entertainment, and operating system software, although large, are beyond the scope of this article.) In addition to being an emerging industry, it is highly fragmented. Out of total 1982 software sales valued at $1.0 billion (retail), only Radio Shack had factory sales over $50 million and fewer than a dozen firms had sales of $10 million or more.

Because of its newness and the proliferation of competitors, this industry is characterized by uncertainty, especially in the areas of technology  and overall business strategy. Technically, there are user (and vendor) questions about which products are the best or most efficient. Strategically, no "right" way of conducting business has been established. Sub-optimal or "wrong" approaches in both areas are masked by the industry's spectacular growth. While these conditions create an opportunity for a new entrant to try out a new product or marketing approach, uncertainty is not equivalent to chaos. Some general application programs, such as "VisiCalc," have been highly successful and have created de facto standards by which other new products are evaluated.

In addition to uncertainty, the software industry exhibits other structural characteristics.[3] Overall entry barriers are low, so low that a large cottage industry of independent software publishers exists. Capital requirements, currently modest, are steadily increasing. Few firms are large enough to take advantage of economies of scale, and there is no established learning curve. There is substantial product turnover because of new entrants and limited (18-36 month) product life cycles.

In such an industry, there are several potentially successful business strategies. Cost minimization approaches include highly centralized management with local execution, e.g., Radio Shack, and formula facilities, e.g., Computerland. Product differentiation strategies attempt to build brand loyalty via promotion, product quality, service support, maximizing apparent value-added or other means. IBM is an example of this approach. Focused strategies concentrate on particular market segments. This is the strategy recommended to a new entrant because it can maximize the firm's return on its (usually) limited resources.

---

[3]Future Computing, Inc., Richardson, Texas. Of course, all estimates of market size, growth rate, market shares, etc., represent the best guess of various market researchers. In an emerging industry, no one really knows today's quantities, much less their future values.'

[4]Our discussion of industry structure and generic strategies utilizes the framework presented by Michael Porter in Competitive Strategy (New York: Free Press, 1980).

For the small firm, the best opportunities appear to lie in vertical markets where the background or insight of company principals can lead to differentiable products which address a using industry's specific needs. These niche markets, although smaller than business-wide applications, are less likely to attract the larger competitors, at least for the time being. A truly innovative approach may even define a new market segment, and the developer may enjoy a temporary near-monopoly position. It is certainly true in the software industry that success breeds imitation, and with the industry's low entry barriers, no firm will enjoy monopoly profits for long. Sources of potential competition include the hardware manufacturers, turnkey system suppliers, computer stores taking a stab at developing their own software, software brokers, and user groups, in addition to the established software houses.

## Critical Factors for Success

It is very easy to get into the software business. All one needs is a product idea, some programming skills, and money. Unfortunately, it is very difficult to be successful in this business. Overall success rates for new product ideas introduced in more established industries are estimated at one-to-five percent. It is probably lower in the software industry. The critical factors for success identified in the authors' investigation were marketing skills and the money to buy or apply them. These marketing factors are discussed below under the traditional four P's: promotion, place, product, and price.

## Promotion

There are literally thousands of new computer-related products, including software, being introduced monthly. How can the new entrant get anyone to pay attention to their program? The promotional tools most commonly mentioned in the survey included the following:

    Dealer or distributor sales kits,
    Dealer support, both sales and technical,
    Shared cost local advertising,
    Trade magazine advertising,
    Dealer promotions.

No survey participant used the mass media to promote their products. Cost and difficulty in reaching targeted users were the major reasons cited. The companies surveyed spent from three to twenty percent of their sales revenues on promotional activities. At the retail level, these firms are simply trying to buy dealer shelf space and some point-of-purchase sales effort.

## Place, or Channels of Distribution

All survey companies used distributors and dealers to market their products. These relationships are usually non-exclusive, i.e., the firm reserves the right to appoint other distributors or dealers in the same territory, although for practical reasons, this may not be done. In addition, most companies reserve the right to sell their products directly to end users. Two firms sold software to hardware manufacturers (OEMs, or Original Equipment Manufacturers) to build into their systems. All participants said their target markets were international, as well as domestic, although only two firms were actually marketing their software overseas.

Only one firm had a dedicated sales force that called directly on computer stores and mass merchandisers. Most firms cannot afford this, so company executives and inside sales people do most of the selling. This is not meant to denigrate the importance of the sales effort. In fact, just the opposite is true. Top level involvement and some "bare knuckle" sales skills appear critical to success.

Today, the channels of distribution can be characterized as "clogged," with too many unsophisticated salespeople at the retail end of the pipe. This will change quickly. Either the middlemen will become more efficient, or more software firms will deal directly with end users. The electronic distribution of products via telecommunication links will facilitate the latter strategy. Most industry analysts and survey participants agree that electronic distribution will dramatically change software marketing strategies. Merchandising will become more sophisticated and directed at end users who will be targeted ever more precisely.

## Product

The survey indicates that even a mediocre product can achieve market success. A technology-oriented firm that spends its limited resources developing the "perfect" product may not be as successful as a firm that spends this money developing marketing tools. Most users cannot tell a "B-" product from an "A" offering. "Bugs" in the initial version of a product appear to be an accepted fact of life. However, failure to fix program problems is not acceptable. Thus, one way a firm can differentiate itself is in program support. In a similar vein, users are becoming increasingly demanding as regards program documentation. Incomplete, shabby, user hostile, and outright wrong documentation are no longer acceptable to even the neophyte buyer.

Product characteristics most important to more sophisticated users include simplicity, flexibility, and demonstrated saving of internal resources.[5] Simplicity

[5]DataPro Research Corporation, Delmar, NJ. Partial results from a 1982 end user survey conducted by DataPro, McGraw-Hill Research, and Computerworld magazine.'

translates to ease of use or user friendliness. Flexibility means the ability to adapt the program to the using firm's needs and systems, rather than vice versa. Savings can appear in two areas: reduced cost when older methods are replaced by the new, and the opportunity costs associated with freeing up inhouse programming resources.

Program piracy, or illegal copying, can rob a new firm of the revenues it needs to survive. All legal (copyrights, licenses, lawsuits, etc.) and technical (copy protection) tools should be used to minimize these losses. Unfortunately, the problem is not going to just "go away," and any firm entering this business must accept this risk. The most effective current strategy appears to be frequent program updates and denial of service support to other than registered owners.

## Price

Typically volume discounts, whether to distributors or end users, are offered. So are such price incentives as cash discounts for prompt payment. But business and technical software is not currently subject to the same downward price pressures as entertainment or home productivity software. The business customer, as the field research and industry data reveal, is usually making software acquisitions for defensive purposes, i.e., maintaining the firm's position vis-a-vis competitors. As a consequence, these customers are less price sensitive, but as noted above, they are very service sensitive. After all, "broken" or malfunctioning programs can lead to a competitive disadvantage for a user.

This relative price insensitivity is a major reason for recommending that a potential entrant consider business or technical vertical markets. It is much easier to protect profit margins, and thus generate resources for further product or market development, not to mention profits, in these areas.

While these end users may not be terribly price sensitive, both they and distribution middlemen are extremely discount sensitive. It is a fact of business life that everybody wants a price advantage. Discounts are either customary or considered part of getting a good deal. Typical discounts from retail prices are 0% to 15% for end users, 20% to 40% for dealers, and 30% to 50% for distributors, with specific values dependent upon volume of products purchased.

## Applying the Four Ps: Eight Steps to Success

How could a new firm use the information presented above to maximize its chances for success? One possible scenario follows. The firm is imaginary, but the suggestions are concrete. It is assumed the firm has no background in the software industry and has limited financial resources. It does have one partially developed product. This firm's overall goal is survival. Its major suggested strategies and tactics are the following.

1. Establish product "ownership" early on. This can easily be overlooked, even in the one-product firm. It is essential that someone be responsible for the product's ultimate success or failure.

2. Make the best use of initial resources by subordinating package graphics to thorough documentation. Spend scarce promotion money where it does the most good.

3. Price the product comparable to competitive products. Ideally, there will be no direct competition, in which case price the product based on the savings users will realize. Accept the reality of discounts. Buyers like to win when discussing prices.

4. Establish realistic short-term objectives for customer contacts, channel development, and product sales. Maintain performance statistics in these areas and measure progress against specific targets.

5. As soon as the product works, get it into users' hands. Be prepared to provide the necessary training and support services. Be responsive and fix bugs quickly. This is the single most important thing to ensure product viability, customer loyalty, and the firm's credibility.

6. Maximize intermediate-term (6-12 months) cash flow by exploring all possible methods and channels of distribution, including the outright sale of the program to a third party.

7. Plow early revenues into promotional efforts, customer service, and product enhancement (including debugging).

8. As soon as the first product is debugged, begin work on the firm's (previously conceptualized) new products to expand the product lines.

## Conclusion

This article has mapped out the competitive environment of the business and technical applications software industry. Key success factors were identified and a basic strategy outlined for a would-be industry participant. This emerging, fragmented industry is clearly a land of opportunity for an individual or small firm with little capital, some technical ability, marketing know-how, and insight into solving day-to-day business problems using the microcomputer.

With the proliferation of new industries such as the software industry and the exponential growth of their markets, it is well to look back at the marketing basics. New products need solid, tried concepts of marketing as described in this study. Highly popular growth products can make it for a while on novelty alone, but eventually marketing fundamentals are necessary for success.

# Successful Business Library

**The Loan Package**
Emmett Ramey and Alex Wong . . . . . . . . . . . . . . . . . . . . . $33.95

**How to Select a Business Computer**
Billie J. Cayot, et al. . . . . . . . . . . . . . . . . . . . . . $33.95

**Develop Your Business Plan**
Richard Leza and Jose Placencia . . . . . . . . . . . . . . . . $33.95

**A Company Policy and Personnel Workbook**
Ardella R. Ramey and Ronald A. Mrozek . . . . . . . . . . . . $33.95

**Getting the Most from Your Business Insurance**
Gary Robinson . . . . . . . . . . . . . . . . . . . . . . . . . $33.95

**Managing People**
Byron D. Lane . . . . . . . . . . . . . . . . . . . . . . . . . $33.95

**Publicity and Public Relations Guide for Business**
Bruce A. Brough . . . . . . . . . . . . . . . . . . . . . . . $33.95

**Marketing Your Products and Services Successfully**
Harriet Stephenson and Dorothy Otterson . . . . . . . . . . . $33.95

**Venture Capital Proposal Package**
Wyman N. Bravard and David B. Frigstad. . . . . . . . . . . . $33.95

**Negotiating the Purchase or Sale of a Business**
James Comiskey . . . . . . . . . . . . . . . . . . . . . . . $33.95

**Staffing a Small Business: Hiring, Compensating and Evaluating**
Robert Worthington and Anita Worthington . . . . . . . . . . $33.95

**Proposal Development: A Winning Approach**
Bud Porter-Roth . . . . . . . . . . . . . . . . . . . . . . . $33.95

**Mail Order Legal Manual**
Erwin J. Keup . . . . . . . . . . . . . . . . . . . . . . . . $45.00

**Career Builder**
W.E. McLeod and Ann Porter-Roth . . . . . . . . . . . . . . . $33.95

**Preventing Crime in Small Business**
Douglas L. Clark . . . . . . . . . . . . . . . . . . . . . . . $33.95

## Software

**For use with Starting and Operating a Business series ...**
CASHPLAN (IBM PC and compatibles—no other software needed) . . . $39.95

**For use with Develop Your Business Plan**
Disk for Lotus 1-2-3 or JAZZ (for IBM PC, compatibles & Macintosh) $39.95

**For use with Corporation books** (for IBM PC & compatibles—includes
word processing program similar to Wordstar) . . . . . . . . . . . $39.95

**For use with A Company Policy and Personnel Workbook**
(IBM PC and compatibles—includes a word processing program also). . . $39.95

**Wall $treet Raider** ... a stock market financial simulation . . . . . . . . $39.95

# Successful Business Library
## Oasis Press
720 South Hillview Drive
Milpitas, CA 95035

**Starting and Operating a Business in** . . . . . .

Authors: Michael D. Jenkins
and co-authors from each of the states
listed. Often the co-authors are associated
with the accounting firm of Arthur Young
and Company.

$26.95 each

| | |
|---|---|
| California | Massachusetts |
| Colorado | New Jersey |
| Florida | New York |
| Georgia | Ohio |
| Illinois | Oklahoma |
| Indiana | Pennsylvania |
| Kansas | Texas |
| Louisiana | Washington |
| Connecticut | Alabama |
| Arizona | Missouri |
| Virginia | West Virginia |
| Maryland | Michigan |
| Tennessee | Arkansas |

**Available in 1986 & 87** . . . . . . . . . . .

| | |
|---|---|
| Nevada | Utah |
| Iowa | New Mexico |
| North Carolina | Kentucky |
| South Carolina | Wisconsin |
| | Minnesota |

**Corporation Startup Package & Minute Books.** .
$33.95 each

| | |
|---|---|
| California | Colorado |
| Delaware | Florida |
| Texas | |

| Title | Price | Qty | Total |
|---|---|---|---|
| | | | |
| | | | |
| | | | |

Subtotal _____
(Calif. residents 7% Sales Tax) _____
Total _____

**Oasis Press**
**Toll-free order phone**

**1-800-228-2275**

**In Calif**
**1-800-221-4089**

__ Check enclosed (postage paid)
__ Charge to __ VISA __ Mastercard __ American Express (shipping added)

Card # _____ Expires _____ / _____ /

Name as shown on card _____

Signature _____

**(We ship via UPS so please give a street address rather than a P.O. box)**

Ship to _____ Title _____

Company _____

Address _____

City _____ State _____ Zip _____